# Growing In God's Family

# GROWING IN GOD'S FAMILY

## *Donald Bridge and*
## *David Phypers*

**HODDER AND STOUGHTON**
LONDON SYDNEY AUCKLAND TORONTO

The verses from *When We Were Very Young* by A. A. Milne are quoted by permission of Methuen Children's Books (UK) and McClelland and Stewart Limited, Toronto.

**British Library Cataloguing in Publication Data**

Bridge, Donald
  Growing in God's family.
  1. Christian life
  I. Title.    II: Phypers, David
  248.4    BV4501.2

ISBN 0 340 34250 1

Hodder and Stoughton Editorial Office: 47 Bedford Square, London WC1B 3DP.

# CONTENTS

# CHAPTER 1 – NEW BIRTH

Jane awoke with a start and lay uneasily in the darkened room.

She glanced across at the glowing digits of the bedside clock – 2.02. By her side John was heavily asleep. Suddenly, the pain came again. Jane caught her breath and stifled a cry. The pain eased, and she lay still and quiet. This must be the time; so long anticipated and now unbelievably here. The baby was on its way. She thought of John and their first meeting five years before. She recalled their happy days of growing love. She remembered the wedding day. She recalled that lovely afternoon, just eight months before, when the doctor had confirmed that she was expecting her first child.

Again the pain leapt upon her; 2.34 said the bedside clock. Time for action. 'John. It's the baby. It's on its way.'

Ambulance, hospital, nurses, doctors, gowned figures around the delivery room table, John's presence, worried yet reassuring, murmured instructions: the memory of those next few hours would always be blurred in Jane's mind. Finally came that moment of inexpressible joy when she held her new-born child safe in her arms, felt the warmth of its tiny body against her own, nuzzled her lips against its infant cheek. And John shared her joy. Years of love and hard work, months of waiting and preparation had borne fruit. Now they were three.

Birth and death are the two great experiences shared by us all. At birth our independent existence begins. We enter conscious life. At the moment of our birth we already carry, within a tiny helpless body, the potential and the promise of all that we shall ever be; the power too, for life itself is the most stubborn and persistent of powers. Few births make the newspaper headlines and the television newscasts. For that, our parents need to be royalty, entertainment stars or notorious criminals! But every birth is a breath-taking miracle of fulfilment and potential.

*Becoming a Christian is like a re-run of being born.* The Bible describes it as being 'born again', 'born anew', 'born from above' and 'born of God'. One night a respected Jewish leader arranged an interview with Jesus. He expected an airy discussion about theology. To his bewilderment, Jesus almost brushed him off. 'I am telling you the truth: no one can see the Kingdom of God unless he is born again' (John 3: 3). Unless you get this straight there is nothing to discuss, Jesus seemed to be saying. Until this happens to you, you will never even see what I have come to do, let alone experience it.

A Christian is someone who has been born twice. The first birth was physical, from human parents. The second birth is spiritual, and the Spirit of God is its source (John 3: 5-8). People often fail to grasp this. They use the word Christian as a cultural word, meaning someone brought up in a certain country. Or they see it as a word of approval, like 'gentleman' or 'good sport'. Others give it a more religious flavour, linking it with rites and ceremonies. Others link it in their minds with self-effort and a certain standard of behaviour. More still see it as assent to a creed, or agreement with a collection of beliefs. But the Bible speaks of something much more radical. A Christian is a person to whom something utterly astonishing has happened. He has been given a new life. His natural life has been invaded by the supernatural. God has given him something. It is something so unique and so priceless that he could not earn it, deserve it, discover it or attain to it; he simply receives it.

The new birth involves a *change of condition*, passing from death to life. Everyone has a physical life, an emotional life, an intellectual life. But spiritual life is something quite different. The friendship of God, the enjoyment of prayer, the discovery of the reason for which we were created, even appetite for things spiritual: all of these are missing – indeed, they are 'dead' – until we are born again (Eph. 2: 1). Then everything changes.

It involves a *change of status*. In contrast to much vague popular thinking, the Bible does not teach that God is the Father of everyone, regardless of who and what we are. Our natural condition is to be suspicious of God, hostile to God, at odds with him – perhaps acknowledging that he may exist but keeping him carefully at arm's length.

To some people Jesus said bluntly 'If God really were your Father, you would love me . . . you are the children of your father, the Devil' (John 8: 42-4). Far from being an automatic accompaniment of being human, the knowledge of the Fatherhood of God is a glorious privilege offered to those who want it sufficiently. 'See how much the Father has loved us! His love is so great that we are called God's children . . . This is why the world does not know us: it has not known God' (1 John 3: 1).

It involves a *change of relationship*. For God has other sons and daughters too – crowds of them! Being born again throws us into a new situation where we have numberless relatives to get to know, relationships to explore, implications to work out. 'Whoever loves God must love his brother also. Whoever believes that Jesus is the Messiah is a child of God; and whoever loves a father loves his child also' (1 John 4: 21 and 5: 1).

It involves a *change of verdict*. During the Korean War a guerrilla fighter murdered the son of a Christian pastor in order to undermine the Christian influence in the village. Later he was captured and put on trial, the grief-stricken father giving evidence against him. But then, to everyone's amazement the pastor pleaded for the life of the murderer of his son. He offered to adopt him. In the confusions of warfare, it was permitted. As a consequence the guerrilla in turn became a Christian. The pastor had turned his verdict of 'guilty' into a verdict of 'accepted'. His stunning act of grace was only a reflection of what God has done for every

Christian. For God takes people who were enemies, rebels, the cause of the death of his Son, and welcomes them into his own family in a relationship of forgiveness, love and trust.

Here is the very heart and core of the Christian Gospel, and the starting-place of everything that Christian living involves. 'God's Spirit joins himself to our spirits to declare that we are God's children' (Rom. 8: 16).

'If you want to judge how well a person understands Christianity,' writes a modern theologian, 'find out how much he makes of the thought of being God's child, and having God as his Father. If this is not the thought that prompts and controls his ... whole outlook on life, it means that he does not understand Christianity very well at all.' (J.I. Packer, *Knowing God*, Hodder.)

'I am a child of God!' cried a vicar in a Home Counties industrial town. The discovery changed him, his church, and, in time, the lives of hundreds of thousands of people around the world (Colin Urquhart, *When the Spirit Comes*, Hodder).

Whenever the Christian church is renewed and revived, this great central fact is discovered.

> Oh, how shall I the goodness tell,
> Father, which thou to me hast showed,
> That I, a child of wrath and hell,
> Should now be called a child of God?

So wrote Charles Wesley, 200 years ago, in the great forward surge of the Evangelical Awakening.

So today, as the spiritual tide turns, a new generation of Christians exploring the wealth of the Gospel, sings,

> We are heirs of the Father,
> We are joint-heirs with the Son,
> We are children of the Kingdom,
> We are family, we are one!

This is a book, not about the *process* of the new birth, but about its *possibilities*. Where does it lead? The new birth itself comes in a variety of ways. Some can name the day –

even the moment – when it happened. Others can simply look back over a period of time and say, '*Then* I knew nothing of it: *now* I believe and enjoy it; somewhere along the road between, it has come to me.' For some it comes as a dramatic crisis and confrontation, demanding a drastic turning from colourful misbehaviour or radical unbelief. For others it presents itself as a gradual awakening under the influence of truth and teaching and example, until the defences against it are almost unconsciously undermined. What matters is not *when* it happened or *how* it happened, but *whether* it has happened. After all, what matters about my natural birth is not so much the date of my birthday, but that fact that I am alive and know who I am! To know that I am alive, I do not need to remember my birth (my parents will remember it well enough!) – what I must do is get on with living.

So with the new birth. It comes in a variety of ways. Jesus said so. 'The wind blows wherever it wishes; you hear the sound it makes, but you do not know where it comes from or where it is going. It is like that with everyone who is born of the Spirit' (John 3: 8). This book is to help you, after you are born into God's family, to get on with living.

# CHAPTER 2 – GROWING UP

John's and Jane's child was welcomed and loved. From the moment he was born he found food, shelter, security and love. Without food and shelter he would quickly have died. Without security and love his mind and emotions would have suffered. In other words, he had a home and was born into a genuine family.

Christians are born into a family too. Without it, they cannot survive. The Christian family is called the church. The church is not so much the building on the corner, or a national or international organisation like the Church of England or the Roman Catholic Church. The church is essentially the whole company of people world-wide who worship Jesus Christ as Saviour and Lord. Because God is their Father they are all brothers and sisters to each other.

The whole church world-wide is made up of many parts, individual churches uniting Christian believers in worship and service. Unfortunately, many Christians find it hard to relate to the church. When they go to a church, they feel unwelcome. They find the proceedings boring. The language used is old-fashioned and out of date. Worse still, many church people are hypocrites, always quarrelling and squabbling, no better than anyone else.

Part of the problem lies in the fact that, in contrast to the population as a whole, Christians in Britain today are at the end of a 150-year period of numerical decline. Many are demoralised and weak. Many have lost their sense of 'the glorious freedom of the children of God' (Rom. 8: 21). Embattled in cold, gloomy buildings with old-fashioned traditions, many congregations struggle on, curious relics of a bygone age.

The picture, however, is not entirely bleak. God's Spirit is at work, bringing new life to many churches as well as to individuals. Many are filled with eager worshippers. Many are active in the wider community, witnessing and bringing others to Christ.

For all their love, John and Jane were imperfect parents, yet their child still needed the warmth and protection they could provide. In the same way, for all its faults, Christians need the church. If they despise it, their faith grows weak, and eventually their new life in Jesus withers.

## What is the church?

When the apostle Paul wrote to his Christian friends in Corinth he addressed his letter 'To the church of God which is in Corinth .... together with all people everywhere who worship our Lord Jesus Christ' (1 Cor. 1: 2). That is the church, the company of all people everywhere who worship Jesus as Lord. Jesus said, 'where two or three come together in my name, I am there with them' (Matt. 18: 20).

So the church is where Jesus is. This glorious fact makes a Christian congregation totally different from any other grouping of people, religious or secular, in the whole world. The church is not a collection of people who have some interest in common, like a sports club, a charity, a study circle, a hobby society or whatever. Nor is it even an association of religious people who admire Jesus, read his sayings and try to follow his example.

The Christian church is a body of people who know the unique, supernatural experience of Jesus with them. As an old hymn says, 'With joy we come to meet our Lord.' This constitutes a church. Without it there is no church. With it the precise details are only incidentals. There may be stained-glass windows and a robed choir. There may be plain wooden forms and a piano. The man at the front may be splendidly attired or may wear jeans and a tee-shirt. The music may swell from a pipe organ or throb from a guitar.

The communion bread and wine may be offered at a rail to kneeling worshippers or passed informally amongst seated friends. What makes the gathering truly Christian, what constitutes the church is the presence of Jesus.

## Why do I need the church so much?

Because Christians are brothers and sisters, joined by their faith in Jesus to God their Father, they naturally need each other. A growing son who never sleeps at home, never speaks to his parents or other members of the family, makes no contribution to the family budget and has no interest in family concerns is quite simply a bad member of the family. In the same way Christians who never bother with church life are bad members of the family of God.

In the church, Christians find affection. Growing children need the warmth of human love if they are to become whole and mature adults. In the same way Christians must love each other if they are to grow strong in their Christian lives. That love they will find and share in the company of the church. 'We know that we have left death and come over into life; we know it because we love our brothers,' wrote the apostle John (1 John 3: 14); 'love one another earnestly with all your heart,' wrote Peter in the same way (1 Pet. 1: 22).

Brothers and sisters cannot choose each other, or their cousins and other relatives either. Yet in a strong family they all learn to love each other despite obvious differences of outlook and temperament. So Christians must love each other despite similar differences. Their differences not only reflect their varying character, but the social strata from which they come and various nationalities from which they are drawn. At a practical level Christians often fail here, only mixing with their own kind, but in Christ they can learn to love all their brothers and sisters throughout the world.

In a strong family, brothers and sisters learn to care for each other. Practical care has always been a hallmark of the Christian church. The infant church in the New Testament

15

was actively engaged in famine relief and in the ongoing support of widows. In later times Christians pioneered hospitals, campaigned for prison reform, developed universal education and tackled the awesome problems of child prostitution and homelessness in the expanding industrial cities of Western Europe. Overseas, Christians and Christians alone have cared for lepers, housed orphans and taught subsistence farmers improved techniques of planting and growing. For all its faults the Christian church is a caring church, and individual Christians have always found care within its doors. Personal problems can be discussed, prayer offered and practical help given and received in a score of ways. 'Help to carry one another's burdens,' wrote Paul, 'and in this way you will obey the law of Christ' (Gal. 6: 2).

Along with care goes dependence. The Western family of father, mother and one or two children is very untypical compared with the family world-wide. There the extended family is much more common. All the members depend on one another, parents, children, uncles, cousins and grandparents. Each has a distinct place, a definite role, a different job to do. The men earn the money. The women raise the children and often do separate work about the home. Older sisters nurse younger children. One son learns a craft from his father, another goes off to hunt. Grandparents pass on traditions and lore.

So in the extended family of the church each Christian has a part to play and all the others depend on him or her for that. Through their natural talents and the special gifts which the Spirit gives to each one, all Christians have a place and a share in the church's life and witness. The guitarist and the organist, the preacher and the singer, the Sunday School teacher and the elder, the personal worker and the secretary: all are needed. The noisy zeal of youth and the mature experience of age, the restless reaching out for more conversions and the solid teaching which guides to maturity, the enthusiasm of the charismatic and the sober reverence of the traditional worshipper of God; all are needed. The apostle and prophet, the evangelist and teacher, the one who gives a message in tongues and the one who interprets that message, the one with ability to heal the sick and the one with the power to discern the activity of spirits; all are needed. Whoever you are, whatever your background, when you are a child of God through faith in Jesus Christ, there is a place for you in His church on which others will depend.


## What should happen in the church?

Two thousand years ago in Jerusalem, during the Jewish festival of Pentecost, the Christian church was born. Filled with the Spirit, the apostle Peter explained to a hushed crowd in the Temple precincts the meaning and purpose of the death and resurrection of Jesus. As a result, 3,000 people were baptised in Jesus's name; the history of the church had begun.

The Bible tells us that these first Christians 'spent their time in learning from the apostles' (Acts 2: 42). That should still be a priority in the church; teaching and learning about Jesus. If Christians are going to follow Christ they need to know what he said and did, and they need to know how his life and teaching were applied by his closest followers, the disciples themselves. In other words, churches should teach their members the contents of the Bible in general and the New Testament in particular. And Christians should be glad to learn the content and meaning of their faith.

The earliest Christians also spent their time 'taking part in the fellowship' (Acts 2:42). In other words they shared together. Their degree of sharing was quite unusual. They 'shared their belongings with one another. They would sell their property and possessions, and distribute the money among all, according to what each one needed' (Acts 2: 44,45). They also shared their homes together. 'They had their meals together in their homes,' we are told (Acts 2: 46). These Christians loved each other so much and were so conscious of their common son-ship in Christ they just loved to be together. As true members of one family they could not

17

bear to see any of their brothers and sisters in need. 'No one said that any of his belongings was his own, but they all shared with one another everything they had' (Acts 4: 32).

Not every modern church reaches that standard. Someone has described many English church members as 'billiard-ball Christians'. They collide briefly on a Sunday, go click-click-click, and scurry back to the safety of individual homes and lives. Sometimes that is so. None the less, there is a generosity among many Christians which is rarely found outside the ranks of the church. To prove it, try comparing the results of a house-to-house collection for charity with the results of a special offering in a church service!

There are many, many churches which display a sharing of life's problems and solutions, its joys and its sorrows, at a level almost unknown in the hard, uncaring, faceless world outside. Garden tools loaned, cars borrowed, lifts to hospital arranged, odd jobs done, inexpensive holidays fixed, baby-sitting laid on, sick-nursing arranged, flowers delivered, notes of sympathy dropped in – a hundred simple signs indicate a shared life which is real and practical. Colin fell off his motor-cycle while travelling up the M1 and ended up in hospital miles from home. A simple appeal in the Sunday morning service at a near-by church for a temporary home for his fiancée to stay and visit him produced a ready response from more than one worshipper. A home was opened to a total stranger, and Christians, previously unknown to each other shared together in a time of crisis. There was nothing special or noteworthy about this; it was part of the church's natural fellowship.

In the church Christians learn to give some of their money to the needs of the church, of the poor and the underprivileged at home and overseas. Ten per cent is a common standard and some give more. In some churches, some Christians are recapturing the total sharing described in the Acts of the Apostles. Fully committed to each other, they share their homes and belongings together, often to enable one or more of them to give themselves in complete service to Jesus Christ.

Two thousand years ago the Jerusalem Christians 'devoted themselves ... to the breaking of bread and the prayers' (Acts 2: 42 RSV). In other words they worshipped together. They remembered Jesus in his death and they constantly brought their needs to him. Their worship was powerful and alive. Tongues of fire and the sound of a strong wind blowing accompanied its first expression. They praised God in other languages, as the Spirit enabled them to speak (Acts 2: 1-4). On one occasion the place where they were meeting was shaken (Acts 4: 31). What a contrast to the desultory, old-fashioned, boring activity which passes for Christian worship in so many churches today! But where the wind of the Spirit is blowing again, worship is once more becoming an immediate, living thing.

In their worship, the earliest Christians remembered Jesus in his death and resurrection. That was the point of their breaking bread together. The last thing Jesus had done before his death had been to break bread and drink wine with his disciples. 'This is my body, which is given for you,' he had said as he had shared the bread among them. 'Do this in memory of me.' And as he passed the cup of wine round the table he had said, 'This cup is God's new covenant sealed with my blood, which is poured out for you' (Luke 22: 19, 20).

The Lord's Supper, Holy Communion, the Eucharist, Breaking the Bread (call it what you will), is still the central act of worship among Christians. Here they praise God for His mighty power and goodness, here they receive instruction in His word, here they bring their prayers together to God's throne, confess their sins, and share God's peace with one another. In the Communion service, Christians on earth are united with Christians in heaven in their eternal praise of Jesus for making them his children and bringing them to glory. The repetition of Christ's words at the Last Supper, the broken bread and the poured-out wine proclaim his death until he comes (1 Cor. 11: 26). And in the actual act of communion, when believers receive the bread and wine, Christ is somehow specially present by his Spirit, and as they receive, they feed on him in their hearts by faith with thanksgiving.

One or two Christian groups have dispensed with the Communion service in their worship. They are poorer as a result. For Jesus told us, as often as we eat bread and drink wine, to do so in remembrance of him. Some Christians rarely receive communion, feeling somehow they are not worthy. But no one is worthy. Jesus alone is worthy and he invites us to come. The table is his; we should not despise his invitation.

The Jerusalem Christians worshipped at two levels: in the Temple and in their homes. That pattern is still the best today. In many churches Christians worship together in the church building for Sunday service and other special occasions, but they also meet with increasing frequency in their homes. There, in small groups, they can pray freely together and bring their particular contributions to the worship in a way which is quite impossible in the larger, more formal gathering.

Because the earliest Christians learned, shared and worshipped together in the power of the Holy Spirit, they were able to reach out to the wider community with the good news of Jesus. Miracles and wonders were an ongoing feature of their life. Their growth-rate was dramatic. 'Every day the Lord added to their group those who were being saved' (Acts 2: 47).

Many of the miracles were for the benefit of those outside the membership: a lame man at the Beautiful Gate of the Temple, sick people carried into the streets to catch Peter's shadow as he passed by, crowds from the towns around Jerusalem bringing those who were ill or who had evil spirits in them, 'and they were all healed' (Acts 5: 16). When the church demonstrated the power and compassion of the living Christ towards those in need, growth followed naturally, as people took a closer look.

*To which church should I belong?*

Many reading this book will probably have connections with a particular Christian community already. The friendship of that church will be their obvious starting-point for their growth as Christians. If you can do so without seriously damaging your hope of progress, stay with the church with which you are already associated. Do not launch out on a quest for a perfect church. They are very thin on the ground. If you find a perfect one and then join it, you will promptly spoil it!

If you are starting the Christian life without the benefit of a previous church link, you will have to make some kind of choice, and the variety can be bewildering. Some set great store by tradition. They find their sense of security and certainty in that things are done and said in a certain way because it has been so for a very long time. The first six centuries of the Christian church make special appeal to such Christians. They use processions, candles and incense in their worship. Their ministers wear elaborate robes or vestments. The people express their devotions in kneeling, standing, bowing and crossing themselves at appropriate times. It is possible to mock them by playfully pointing out that Roman clothes, medieval ceremonies, Elizabethan words, Gothic buildings and Victorian tunes do not exactly conspire to announce that God is alive in the twentieth century! They would respond with spirit that they are not meant to. It is the unchanging nature of God and the reality of his grace down through the centuries that is being emphasised. Such churches are usually called Catholic.

Other churches give the Bible a very high place in their public worship. A large copy may be carried in prominently at the beginning. Smaller copies will be available for the worshippers to use. The explanation of Bible passages will be an important feature, and the preaching of the sermon on a scriptural topic or passage will be regarded as the high point of the service. The need for a personal encounter with Jesus Christ is likely to be emphasised. Sharing the faith with others has a high priority. Such churches are usually described as Evangelical.

Others again will have a reputation for being Liberal or Radical. Their concern will be to keep the church up to date, both in belief and behaviour. While valuing the Bible as a source-book of inspiration, they will underrate its authority, and the note of certainty will often be absent from their message.

The Charismatic movement has become a major trend in many churches this century. Charismatic churches (to varying degrees) are marked by spontaneous unstructured worship, informality, and an emphasis on the supernatural. Their expressions of worship are enthusiastic and physical; hand-clapping, uplifting of arms in prayer, clasping of each other's hands, even dancing, may be features of such a church.

What a confusing variety! Anglican, Methodist, Baptist, or whatever ... and then cutting across these groupings, catholics, Evangelical, Liberal, Charismatic, or a mixture. How can I decide? The title on the notice board will tell you little.

First, look for a church with *a Biblically-based ministry*. A church which is concerned to teach, explain and apply the contents of the Bible is a church in which you will grow as a Christian. For the Bible is our only witness to Jesus. In the Bible we learn of him, our Saviour and example. Through the Bible God speaks. As we absorb its teaching and obey its commands we become like Jesus and grow strong in our Christian faith.

Look for a church with *a desire for evangelism* and for lives to be changed by an encounter with Jesus. British Christians are notoriously reticent when it comes to sharing their faith with others. Even the churches that try find it hard to win the lost for Christ, but at least find a church which believes in conversion, which preaches conversion and which looks to the Holy Spirit to change people's lives and bring them from death to life.

Look for a church which encourages and is developing *a*

*shared ministry*. British churches have tended to over-encourage clergy-professionalism. Their ministers are carefully chosen and well trained; and then expected to do a dozen different jobs, some of which do not fit either their own gifts or God's plan. Look for a church where everyone has a part to play, and the ministry of the church in teaching, healing, preaching, evangelising, administration and witnessing is shared among many members.

Look for a church which recognises *the centrality of prayer* in the life of the individual and the congregation. Christians find it hard to pray, but a praying Christian is a growing Christian. Churches find prayer is all too easily squeezed out of their programmes, but praying churches are growing churches. All the zeal in the world, all the best techniques will achieve nothing unless they are covered in prayer and are accomplished in the strength and power of Jesus. The prayer-life may be expressed in many different ways according to various traditions, but its presence will be obvious.

Look for a church and find one. When you find one, stay with it despite its faults and drawbacks. 'A rolling stone gathers no moss', and Christians who drift from church to church are of little use to themselves or others. Without the church, you will die. With it 'we shall become mature people, reaching to the very height of Christ's full stature' (Eph. 4: 13).

# CHAPTER 3 – KEY OF THE DOOR

Twenty-one today! Twenty-one today!
Never been twenty-one before.
Give him, oh give him the key of the door!

At twenty-one British young people used to come of age.
Now it happens at eighteen. Somewhere between eighteen
and twenty-one we grow up. Childhood is finally left behind
and we become adults. Our freedom and independence are
signified by the front-door key; we gain the right to come and
go as we please. Often we have a party too. Friends and
relatives come and share our joy. They give us presents to
mark our entrance into adult life.

Christians come of age too. By God's Spirit we are born
again. By God's grace we are adopted as his children. By
faith in Jesus we pass from death to life. And to mark our
membership of his family, God gives us a key, and with it
many presents. That key is baptism.

Baptism is not a 'must' without which Christian living is
impossible. But it is a very strong 'should' which the Bible
takes for granted in the Christian's progress. Like the key of
the door it represents, symbolises and opens the way to many
of God's gifts for the mature Christian who wants to take his
proper place in the Family. In passing from death to life
without being baptised the dying thief was the exception, not
the rule (Luke 23: 42, 43). The New Testament writers knew
nothing of unbaptised Christians. Nor do we necessarily
have to wait for eighteen or twenty-one years before we can
be baptised. When the Holy Spirit came on Cornelius and
his relatives and friends, Peter ordered them to be baptised

there and then (Acts 10: 44-8). When the Philippian gaoler and his family believed in the Lord Jesus they were baptised before waiting for dawn (Acts 16: 31-4). If we mean to grow and take our full place in the family of God we should be baptised.


## Repentance

Baptism is a picture of our repentance. That is what happens when we are born into God's family. We turn our backs on the past. Life begins all over again. This was John the Baptist's message as he called on the people to prepare themselves for the coming of Jesus. It was also the apostle Peter's message in the first Christian sermon on the Day of Pentecost, 'Each one of you must turn away from his sins and be baptised in the name of Jesus Christ' (Acts 2: 38).

When the earliest Christians were baptised they took off their old clothes before the ceremony and put on new, white robes. Their old clothes symbolised their old way of life which they were leaving behind; their new ones symbolised their new life in Jesus which they were now beginning. So Paul says, 'you have taken off the old self with its habits and have put on the new self' (Col. 3: 9,10).

Now although repentance is something we have to do for ourselves, it is also something which God enables us to do. It is one of God's presents which he gives us when we are born into his family. And so baptism reminds us that the goodness of God leads us to repent (Rom. 2: 4 RSV).


## Forgiveness

When we repent God forgives us and baptism tells us that too. 'Turn away from your sins and be baptised,' said John, 'and God will forgive your sins' (Mark 1: 4). 'Each one of you must turn away from his sins and be baptised in the name of

Jesus Christ,' said Peter, 'so that your sins will be forgiven' (Acts 2: 38).

Forgiveness is one of God's loveliest presents to his children. We do not have to earn it or compensate God for it in any way. He gives it to us freely through our Lord Jesus Christ. Like any gift we simply have to accept it. In baptism we are pronounced forgiven.

Guilt is one of our most depressing and destructive emotions. Real or imagined it can haunt us for years on end. When Herbert joined up as a teenager and went to fight in France during the First World War he was billeted for a while in a civilian home. Its only occupant was a young French woman whose own husband was away fighting on another part of the battle front. Not surprisingly the two were soon sleeping together; when Herbert was moved on his 'landlady' was expecting his child.

Forty years later the memory of that adventure returned to taunt Herbert. It kept him awake at night. It destroyed his concentration at work. What had happened to the woman when her husband had returned, if he ever did? What had happened to the child? Where was he now? There was no way he could ever find out, but he could not forget and his personality fell apart. His English wife of many years freely forgave him his wild oats, but it made no difference. Racked by guilt, Herbert sat at home day after day, totally rejecting everything his wife, his friends, his doctor tried to do to help him.

One night, Herbert told his story to two Christian friends. They told him of Jesus. Before the night was through Herbert accepted Christ and his forgiveness. He walked home with a spring in his step. His guilt was gone; his sin had been washed away.

No sin is too deep for God to forgive. One day, a man was listening to a preacher in Hyde Park. He shyly asked in a foreign accent 'Can God forgive murder?' He went on to describe how he had been caught up in the Hungarian Revolution in 1956. Walking down a city street one winter's afternoon at the height of the disturbances he had seen his boss at work seated at a table in a house with his wife and family. The boss was hated and feared by all the employees for his harsh and unyielding regime. The young Hungarian saw his chance for revenge, pulled two hand grenades from his pocket, hurled them through the window and killed the entire family. Years later, in an Open Air Mission caravan in Hyde Park he found the answer to his question, 'Yes, God can forgive murder.'

Whatever we are, whatever we have done, God forgives us. Baptism is a picture of our forgiveness.


*The Holy Spirit*

When we are baptised God gives us another lovely present, the Holy Spirit. He comes from God the Father and from the Lord Jesus himself to live inside us, to fill us with his power, to make us like Christ, to give us all the strength we need to follow him.

Jesus himself received the Holy Spirit at his baptism. 'As soon as Jesus came up out of the water, he saw heaven opening and the Spirit coming down on him like a dove' (Mark 1: 10). When Peter urged baptism on his Jerusalem audience at Pentecost he promised them, 'and you will receive God's gift, the Holy Spirit' (Acts 2: 38).

Without the Holy Spirit we cannot live for Jesus. He is our constant Helper, he stays with us for ever; he reveals the truth about God, he gives glory to Jesus, he prays for us in sighs too deep for words, he pours out his gifts to make us effective in our service for Jesus and the work of his church, he is our guarantee of final glory and all the joys of heaven for ever.

Right from the beginning the earliest Christians recognised and claimed the gift of the Holy Spirit in baptism. The failure of the Holy Spirit to come to the newly-baptised Christians in Samaria caused Peter and John specifically to pray for and claim this gift (Acts 8: 14-17). When Ananias went to Saul, after his vision of Jesus on the Damascus road, and placed his hands on him so that he might see again and be filled with the Holy Spirit, Saul stood up and was baptised (Acts 9: 17-19). The outpouring of the Holy Spirit on the gathering in Cornelius's home at Caesarea convinced Peter that they should be baptised (Acts 10: 44-8). When the twelve men at Ephesus were baptised in the name of the Lord Jesus, 'Paul placed his hands on them, and the Holy Spirit came upon them' (Acts 19: 6). For this reason, every baptismal service should include the laying-on-of-hands on those who are baptised, and earnest prayer that they may receive the Holy Spirit.

## Faith

Besides all these things, baptism is also an expression of our faith. Faith in Jesus saves – faith alone, but apart from the dying thief and Sergius Paulus, the New Testament tells of no Christian who did not express his or her faith in baptism. An Ethiopian official gave Philip a ride in his chariot as he hitched a lift from Jerusalem to Gaza and listened amazed as Philip explained the scriptures and told him the Good News about Jesus. When he asked, 'Here is some water, what is to keep me from being baptised?' Philip replied, 'You may be baptised if you believe with all your heart' (Acts 8: 36-7 with footnote).

So close is the New Testament link between faith and baptism that sometimes its writers declare that faith saves, and sometimes they declare that baptism saves (1 Pet. 3: 21). They are not contradicting themselves. They are simply expressing the complementary truths that faith without baptism is incomplete, while baptism without faith is meaningless and empty.

Like every other aspect of our coming to Christ, faith is also one of God's gifts. Although we have to believe, God himself enables us so to do. 'It is by God's grace that you

29

have been saved through faith. It is not the result of your own efforts, but God's gift, so that no one can boast about it' (Eph. 2: 8,9).

## Dying and rising with Christ

When we turn our back on sin and begin our new life in Jesus we die and rise with him. As he died on the cross and was raised to new life from the tomb so we die to the past and enter into eternal life. This aspect of our Christian lives is vividly portrayed in baptism. 'By our baptism ... we were buried with him and shared his death, in order that, just as Christ was raised from death by the glorious power of the Father, so also we might live a new life' (Rom. 6: 4).

A baptism is a funeral; not a sad funeral but a happy one. It signifies death to the past, for Christ died for us. It opens the gate on new life for ever as we share Christ's resurrection life. It corresponds with and fulfils the Old Testament ceremony of circumcision. No longer is this a mere physical mark of belonging to a particular, favoured nation, but a spiritual sign that we are freed from the power of our sinful selves (Col. 2: 11, 12). New life in Jesus and freedom from the past are two more lovely presents God gives us at our baptism.

## Membership in the church

When we are baptised into Christ we are also baptised into his church. 'All of us ... have been baptised into the one body,' says Paul (1 Cor. 12: 13). We cannot be Christians without belonging to Christ's church. Every natural child is born into a family. He may be orphaned from his family. His family may be divided and fall apart, but he still belongs to his family. If he does not he suffers inevitably.

So it is with Christians. We cannot become God's children without being born into his family. God's church may be divided. It may be torn apart by deep failure, but it is still his church, and if we follow Christ we belong to it. So baptism, besides being the sign that we belong is also, in a sense, our birth certificate. It admits us to all the rights and privileges of membership of Christ's church. We should not despise baptism and we should not despise the church.

Christ's church does not exist simply on earth; it also exists in heaven. The whole company of believers in earth and heaven makes up the church. The church in worship on earth is united with the church in heaven. The church in heaven is part of our guarantee that we shall join the saints who are already there. And we are washed in baptism so that we might come into possession of the eternal life we hope for (Titus 3: 5-7). Baptism deals with the past and closes it. It looks forward to eternal life for ever.

### 'And to your children'

On the Day of Pentecost, when Peter urged his audience to be baptised, he added a promise which is often forgotten or ignored by modern Christians. 'God's promise,' he said, 'was made to you and your children' (Acts 2: 39).

As a Jew, Peter was fully aware that God includes children in the blessings attached to their parents' faith. When Abraham believed and obeyed God, God vowed to keep his promise to him and to his descendants in future generations forever (Gen. 17: 7-8). King David sang, 'The steadfast love of the Lord is from everlasting to everlasting upon those who fear him, and his righteousness to children's children' (Psalm 103: 17 RSV).

In the birth of Jesus, Mary saw the fulfilment of God's promise to show mercy 'to Abraham and to all his descendants forever' (Luke 1: 55). Therefore, it was the most natural thing in the world for Peter to unite parents and children in the promised gift of the Holy Spirit.

As a Jew, Peter also understood that the ceremony of circumcision expressed this conviction. Jewish children did

31

not have to wait until they grew up and consciously believed in God for themselves before they received the mark of belonging to God's people; they received it in infancy, when they were only eight days old. In this way, Jewish parents accepted God's promises on behalf of their children and signified their obedience to God's covenant with them and their descendants for ever (Gen. 17: 9-14).

Now we have already seen that baptism is the Christian equivalent and fulfilment of circumcision (above p.30 and Col. 2: 11, 12). Because children are included in God's promises to their parents, because they are 'holy' on account of their parents' faith (1 Cor. 7: 14), millions of Christians from the very earliest days of the church have baptised their children as the Jews circumcised theirs.

In the Western half of the church, Christians who have baptised their children have left the ceremony incomplete until the children have become old enough to express their faith for themselves. Then the ceremony has been completed in the process of confirmation when the child renews the baptismal promises made on his behalf by his parents and receives the laying-on-of-hands for the gift of the Holy Spirit. In churches which do not practise confirmation by a bishop, some similar opportunity is nevertheless given to make a verbal confession of faith and to be received as spiritual 'adults' into church membership.

Other Christians have not been so sure. They have argued that the New Testament emphasis on personal faith as the means of salvation places baptism on a new footing. The analogy with circumcision they find unconvincing: only people who consciously believe should be baptised, they maintain. Such baptist Christians have significantly devised 'infant dedication' to express their conviction that their children are not like 'pagan children' but are 'acceptable to God' (1 Cor. 7: 14). This declares what they wish to say about the children of Christians, without confusing it with the baptism of believers.

Christian disagreement on the vexed question of infant baptism has been long and bitter (our *The Water That*

*Divides* has a fuller discussion of the issues involved). Semi-magical views that infant baptism automatically produces eternal salvation without any faith being involved by the parents or, later, by the growing child have not helped. Misguided and mistaken attempts to equate the nation with the church have further confused the issues. The glorious truth that children are included in the blessings which flow from their parents' faith and baptism has all too often been obscured and ignored.

Supporters of both practices (when followed seriously and responsibly) can claim biblical support. Christians should respect their differences in this sensitive area and so all in their power to avoid giving and causing offence, whilst making sure that they faithfully follow their consciences and their understanding of the Bible.

## Types of baptism

Traditionally, Christians have baptised in three ways. They have sprinkled water (baptism by aspersion), poured water (baptism by affusion) and dipped the baptised beneath water (baptism by immersion). Sometimes they have combined these different types of baptism. Occasionally, they have insisted that only one kind of baptism is correct. There are obvious symbolic values to each, and it is against the whole New Testament understanding to make the outward mode a cause of contention.

The use of water in baptism always symbolises the washing away of our sins and God's gift of new life in the Holy Spirit. Baptism by sprinkling reminds us that we have been sprinkled with the blood of Christ (1 Pet. 1: 2). His death on the cross and the shedding of his blood there brings us by faith to the Father.

Baptism by pouring tells us that God has poured out his Holy Spirit on us. It was probably a frequent method used in the New Testament. The baptisms recorded at Pentecost and in the homes of Cornelius and the Philippian gaoler were likely, in the circumstances, to have been by pouring.

Baptism by immersion vividly declares that we have been buried and raised with Christ. It was the method used by John at the River Jordan when he baptised Jesus and by Philip when he baptised the Ethiopian official. It was rapidly adopted by the early church and remains in widespread world-wide use today. Especially when carried out in natural water such as a river or the sea it becomes an effective public declaration of faith in Christ.

## Should I be rebaptised?

If you believe in Jesus and have been born again by his Spirit into the family of God, and if you have never been baptised in the name of the Father, the Son and the Holy Spirit, then you should be baptised as soon as possible. However strong your faith you will find that baptism will make it stronger. Through baptism you will symbolise, receive and strengthen the lovely presents God is waiting to give you.

If you were baptised as a child and have never made your baptismal promises for yourself then you should be confirmed or receive the equivalent as practised in your church. Pray that in the laying-on-of-hands God will fill you with his Spirit in a new way, strengthening your faith, increasing your joy and equipping you with his gifts for his service. Expect it to happen.

But suppose you were baptised as an infant and confirmed as a young teenager, or suppose you were baptised as a teenager and have only now come to a living faith in Christ. Should you now be baptised again as an expression of your new-found faith?

This is not an easy question to answer with a simple rule. We can be born only once into God's family so it follows that true baptism, the symbol of our new birth, can also be given only once. But what exactly is true baptism? God does not always work in the neat and tidy way we should like him to. All the baptisms in the New Testament followed people's

34

faith, but they did not all follow their reception of the Holy Spirit. In the case of the Samaritans, that came later (Acts 8: 14-17), but they did not need another baptism to ratify it. One man in the New Testament, Simon the magician, was baptised by mistake, for his faith was spurious. But we cannot imagine that Peter and John would have baptised him again had he repented as they demanded (Acts 8: 9-24).

What was the intention and the belief expressed in your baptism? Someone almost certainly believed that through it God would honour his promises and in his way and his time would bring us to the living faith that baptism signifies.

If we believe after we have been baptised (and confirmed, for that matter) then we need to renew our vows and give them their full meaning. Many churches make provision for this already. At every baptism service the congregation can be urged to renew their vows as they watch those being baptised. Methodists renew their vows annually in a moving Covenant Service. Perhaps leaders of other services can be asked to introduce similar services of renewal of vows for individuals and for whole congregations where this is felt to be appropriate. Certainly people who have come to a living faith long after their formal baptism and confirmation must have some opportunity of publicly declaring their new-found trust in Jesus.

The key of the door! God's door is open wide for full committed membership in the local church. Inside is the adventure of worshipping God, serving others, learning from fellow Christians and exercising to the full those gifts and talents which God grants to his growing children.

# CHAPTER 4 – LEARNING TOGETHER

Little Brian was very disappointed. For over a year he had been longing to start school. Now the big day had come. Scrubbed face, shiny shoes, socks pulled up, he set off jauntily to the great new learning experience. Five hours later, he returned in tears, socks hanging down, shoes scuffed and face dirty. 'They haven't taught me to read and write!' he sobbed.

Eventually the reading and writing came along, though Brian never quite understood how. In fact, for the next five years his mother's question, 'What did you learn today?' produced the invariable reply, 'The same as yesterday!' It seemed that way because most learning is slow and unselfconscious, 'letter by letter, line by line, lesson by lesson' (Isa. 28: 10).

When we are born into the Christian family God expects us to learn from him. And in order that we may learn he has given us a book. *The Bible*. As we read the Bible so we grow, for it contains material suitable for the newest Christian and for the most advanced. 'Be like new-born babies,' says Peter, 'always thirsty for the pure spiritual milk, so that by drinking it you may grow up and be saved' (1 Pet. 2: 2). The trouble, complains the writer of the Letter to the Hebrews, is that 'you are so slow to understand . . . Instead of eating solid food, you still have to drink milk . . . Let us go forward, then, to mature teaching and leave behind us the first lessons of the Christian message' (Heb. 5: 11-6: 1).

*Why we should read the Bible*

'All Scripture is inspired by God,' says Paul (2 Tim. 3: 16) and this is the main reason why we should read it. Through the Bible God speaks. The Bible is a very human book, bringing together the work of many authors over at least 2,000 years of history. But when they wrote they were 'under the control of the Holy Spirit as they spoke the message that came from God' (2 Pet. 1: 21). And through their writings God still speaks today, to those who will listen.

Then we should read the Bible because it tells us about Jesus. In the four Gospels we find our only reliable information about him. Also the whole Bible is about Jesus. When Jesus said, 'these very Scriptures speak about me!' (John 5: 39) he was of course referring to the first part of the Bible which we call the Old Testament and which was finished 400 years before he was born! But the Old Testament is still about Jesus. It tells us how he was promised from the dawn of history. We learn how Jewish prophets looked forward to his coming, and how they sometimes described him in greater detail than the authors of the four Gospels themselves. Often the lives of Old Testament characters and the events they experienced foreshadowed aspects of the life of Jesus.

The New Testament also is all about Jesus, for his work continues in the life of his church after he was raised and ascended into heaven. In their letters to the young churches of Asia Minor the writers gave basic Christian instruction which is still important today.

When the New Testament authors write about 'the Scriptures' they usually mean the Old Testament. But their own writings were quickly recognised as 'Scriptural' by the early Christians as well (2 Pet. 3: 15, 16). The whole Bible, from Genesis to Revelation, is inspired by God. With the writing of Revelation, God's showing of himself in Jesus was complete, and so the Bible came to an end. We are warned not to add anything, nor to take anything away from what God has said (Rev. 22: 18, 19).

Through the Bible God speaks. In the Bible we learn about Jesus. From the Bible we receive instruction in Christian living. 'All Scripture is inspired by God,' says

Paul, 'and is useful for teaching the truth [what to believe], rebuking error [what not to believe], correcting faults [how to avoid wrongdoing], and giving instruction for right living [how to behave properly]' (2 Tim. 3: 16). This is what we learn from the Bible. And all to what purpose? – 'so that the person who serves God may be fully qualified and equipped to do every kind of good deed' (2 Tim. 3: 17).

When the learning process is complete (if it ever is) we become qualified, as doctors, accountants, plumbers, engineers, computer programmers, hairdressers or whatever. Our qualifications should equip us for every situation we are likely to meet in our chosen profession or occupation. So a knowledge of the Bible qualifies us and equips us to serve God.

Getting to grips with the Bible should therefore be a high priority. If we fail here we are likely to become stunted Christians, never making any real progress in the Christian life.

## How we should not read the Bible

Martin was a merchant seaman. One day, while he was on leave, he looked into the youth club which had kept him entertained in earlier years and decided on the spur of the moment to attend the church that ran it. Before long, his interest stirred, faith began to develop and he became a committed Christian. He was told that the new Christian must begin to grow by reading his Bible. He found the only Bible in his home. It belonged to his mother; a black leather-covered Authorised Version. Over a thousand pages were bound together in double columns and tiny print, in words that had already ceased to be the everyday language of the English people when they were first translated over 350 years ago. Turning to the first page, he began to read.

With commendable determination, Martin struggled through a long and fulsome preface in praise of King James and another long list of largely unpronounceable Contents before he reached *Genesis*, the beginning of the Bible proper. After some difficult chapters about the creation of the world and of the human race, which seemed curiously at odds with what he had learned in dimly-remembered science lessons at school, Martin suddenly found himself absorbed in some fine stories. Even the old-fashioned language became less of a problem as he revelled in some of the greatest literature ever written. Obvious moral and spiritual lessons were being taught as well. People trusted God and launched out on adventures of faith. Their life-style was very different from Martin's but he seized the point without much difficulty.

*Exodus*, the second book in the Bible, proved to be rather similar. The family in the first book had now become a nation. God intervened with tremendous acts of power. The Commandments were given and they made a great deal of sense. Then, all of a sudden, the going became distinctly rough. Martin read a detailed construction plan: 'Thou shalt also make a table of shittim wood ... a cubit and a half the height thereof. And thou shalt overlay it with pure gold and make thereto a crown of gold round about ...'– page after page of that kind of thing.

In fact, Martin had got about as far as most people do when they approach the Bible for the first time and begin at the beginning. He struggled through Exodus and finally became bogged down in Leviticus, in a welter of blood sacrifices, extraordinary ceremonies, and a ritual that bore not the slightest resemblance to the kind of thing that went on in his church.

The trouble was that Martin had approached the Bible as if it were a novel, where you begin at page one and continue, page by page, to the climax at the end. But the Bible is not a novel. It is a collection of sixty-six different kinds of writings, or *books* as they are usually called, assembled over hundreds of years. These writings include history, law-codes, drama, songs, wise sayings and reflections on the meaning of life, sermons, science-fiction-type interpretations of contemporary and future events, biographies and letters. Reading them through, one after the other, is rarely the best way to become acquainted with them. Nor, as Martin found to his cost, is it really practical.

Alice came to the Bible quite differently. Her husband became seriously ill and the local church showed kindness and interest. Before he died, he came into a simple certainty that heaven was for him. After it was all over, Alice found faith growing in her own heart too. She prayed to a God in whom she had always vaguely believed. He became very real and very personal to her as Father and Saviour. She joined the church and discovered that she had indeed come into a new family.

Alice's Bible was an old one too. She noticed that many Christians of her own age loved to quote their favourite passage. She asked to be shown where they were. Soon, she was dipping in for herself, anywhere, as she turned the pages over. And she found some splendid stuff as a result:

'God is our refuge and strength, A very present help in trouble.'

'Trust in the Lord with all thine heart. And lean not unto thine own understanding.

'In all thy ways acknowledge him And he shall direct thy paths.'

'Let not your heart be troubled, neither let it be afraid.'

But the dip-in-at-random method did not work for long. One day Alice read, 'And the fifth angel sounded, and I saw a star fall from heaven unto the earth, and to him was given the key to the bottomless, and there arose a smoke out of the pit, and there came out of the smoke locusts upon the earth.' Whatever was that all about?

Worse was to come. 'That which befalleth the sons of men befalleth beasts, even one thing befalleth them as the one dieth, so dieth the other. Yea, they have all one breath, so that a man hath no pre-eminence above a beast.' No life after death! Is that what it meant? No difference between men and animals! But what about the peace and certainty that Alice's dying husband had found? What about the ringing assurance of life everlasting with which her minister had encouraged her?

41

Alice had made the mistake of reading bits of the Bible without any attempt to understand their original purpose, their context or the cultural setting in which they were first written. Amazingly, although the Bible was written hundreds of years ago in a world which was very different from our own, God continues to speak through its pages. And through the Holy Spirit he can leap across all the hurdles of language, history and culture to touch our hearts today. But God has give us minds of our own as well. When we read the Bible he expects us to use them and to learn as intelligently as we are able. The Bible is not a spiritual pot of gold out of which we can pluck nuggets at will. We are to read it carefully and sensibly if we are to get the best out of it.

Sheila loved to argue with the Bible. As a student-teacher she was openly sceptical of its claims. She sometimes drifted into the college Christian Union to expose it as a sham to these incredulous Christians! Because the Bible was written long ago, when people thought differently and asked different questions from people today, Sheila found plenty to expose. Where did evolution fit into the Biblical account of creation? Whence did Cain obtain his wife? Did God really tell the invading Israelites to commit genocide in Canaan, or the lyricists of the Psalms to call down judgment on their enemies? Surely the accounts of the resurrection were made up to compensate for the Christians' loss of face at his crucifixion! The implicit contradictions in them were proof of that; and so on, and so on.

Because God is the author of the Bible, Sheila cynically expected it to be scientifically infallible, and of course it is not. Some Christians too have tried to find answers to every conceivable question in the Bible. As a result they have ended up believing in a flat earth at the centre of the universe, and a creation date of 4004 BC!

One day Sheila was challenged to read the Bible in a different spirit. What if its claims were true? What if God was the author after all? What if, all the time she had imagined she was judging the Book, the Book was, in fact, judging her? She tried the experiment and it shook her.

42

Before long she was turning to the Bible and the 'wets' in the CU with deep personal questions. Why was I born? What is the point of life? Why is it hard to do right and easy to do wrong? Is God interested in me? How can I be sure? And because she was asking the right questions, the Bible changed her life.

Like Sheila, we have to approach the Bible reverently, for it carries the stamp of God's authority. We must depend on God. Because the Bible deals in spiritual truth, we need spiritual enlightenment. This has nothing to do with whether we are graduate standard, O-level, eleven-plus fail or educationally subnormal.

'Open my eyes, so that I may see the wonderful truths in your law,' (Ps. 119: 18) should be our prayer as we read, whether in church, or privately at home.


*How we should read the Bible*

If we are going to read the Bible profitably, we must learn to read it regularly. Some time every day should be our aim, even if we do not always achieve it. When God is our Father we should want to hear what he has to say. If we never allow him time to speak we cannot complain if he seems distant and remote. So fix a regular time each day when you can spend at least ten to fifteen minutes listening to God from the Bible and replying to him in prayer.

Then we should read the Bible systematically. This way we shall avoid the hazards of the dip-in-at-random approach and the pitfalls of slogging through difficult chapters which never seem to end. For close on a hundred years the Scripture Union has been publishing daily Bible-reading notes for Christians for all ages and stages; we cannot recommend them too highly. *Key Notes* for teenagers, *Daily Bread* for new Christians, and *Daily Notes* for the more mature, all provide a suggested passage for each day with a helpful explanatory comment and an outline prayer as well. Over a five-year period most of the New

43

Testament and much of the Old is covered, so you learn to find your way round the Book as a whole. If you do not like the Scripture Union guides, similar daily notes are published by the International Bible Reading Fellowship, the Crusade for World Revival with *Every Day With Jesus*, and the Salvation Army with *The Soldier's Armoury*. Christian bookshops and church bookstalls usually carry stocks of some if not all of these notes; place your order and start reading.

As we read we should always remember the purpose for which the Bible was written. Does the passage teach something about God? Can we learn anything from it about Jesus? Does it speak about ourselves? Is there a warning to heed, or an example to follow?

When God speaks he calls us to act, so when we read the Bible we should be prepared to obey. Is there something needing to be done as a result of what we have read – an apology to make, a neglected duty to perform, a habit to give up, a decision to take? Through the regular reading of the Bible God can call us to make big choices for him, perhaps involving our job of work or the place where we live. We rarely receive instant guidance in this way and we should always avoid being impulsive, but if we let God speak he will insist on making his way clear.

So we should always read the Bible prayerfully, thanking and praising God for what we have read and praying in any lessons we may have learned. We shall be saying more about prayer in the next chapter; suffice to say here that Bible reading and prayer should always go together. That way we enter into a two-way communication with God.

From time to time we should change our system. Read one of Paul's letters at a sitting, just as you would a letter from a friend. Read a Gospel as you would a modern biography. Try singing some of the Psalms spontaneously! If only you and God can hear no one will be embarrassed!

If you are naturally studious begin to collect other helps to your understanding of the Bible. A one-volume *Commentary* will give a brief outline of each book and explain its general direction. A *Concordance* is an alphabetical word-index. Following through the occurrences of a word like 'Saviour' or 'forgiveness' can often be extremely useful. A *Bible Dictionary* contains articles about Bible books, characters, geography, authors, contemporary history and relevant archaeological discoveries which throw light on Bible passages. All these and other aids will help you to understand references which are often obscure and puzzling to a modern reader. What is a Christian 'yoke', for instance, and why is it 'easy'? How did Peter come to be sleeping on the roof? What was 'the wilderness'? Why should the Good News of Jesus be described as new wine needing a new skin?

As you become more familiar with the Bible try something a little more ambitious. At four chapters a day you can cover the Old Testament once, and the New Testament and Psalms twice in a year! At this pace you will get a grasp of the Bible as a whole and not just of a collection of seemingly disconnected writings.

As well as private reading, we learn with others. When little Brian at last learned to read, he indulged in a lot of private reading. A good book and a warm bed on a winter's night were a delight. Reading almost indiscriminately, he slowly learned by use and comparison the meaning of unfamiliar words and ideas. Sometimes his guesses were ludicrously wrong. For a long time he mentally pronounced 'misled' as if it rhymed with 'sizzled'. For a long time his knowledge of eighteenth-century Europe depended on *The Scarlet Pimpernel*. His ideas of Victorian England were drawn exclusively from Sherlock Holmes. If our reading of the Bible is purely private, we may run into the same kind of problem.

Fortunately he did not depend entirely on private reading. He had formal teaching too. At school there were teachers who knew more than he did, and they passed on their knowledge to him.

The Christian needs to 'go to school' for further Bible knowledge. His school is the local church, and his teachers are those whom God has equipped and appointed to hand on the truth. Formal teaching, in Sunday services and midweek, is one of the chief responsibilities of the vicar, minister or pastor. Many churches have elders or pastoral leaders who share the task. Sitting in a congregation to listen, the Christian submits his mind to Bible truth. Joining in a small group where there can be question and discussion, he learns with others how to hammer out its meaning and apply its lessons. Attendance at one formal 'listening' and one informal 'sharing' is an essential minimum in the weekly learning process. The first on its own can create mere apathetic listeners who do not hear. The second by itself can degenerate into mere shared ignorance. The two together give balance and growth.

Jenny was a middle-aged housewife. Her children went to Sunday School and persuaded her to 'try the church'. She felt welcome and wanted to know more. But the language was a bit technical and the minister took an awful lot of knowledge for granted.

She joined one of the church's groups for housewives. They read a passage of the Bible each week and learned to dig meaning and help out of it. The group leader kept linking what they discovered with the great basic Christian truths.

'I didn't dare ask any questions at first,' Jenny later wrote to the minister. 'I felt so daft that I knew nothing. But often one of the others would ask the very thing that was in my mind. It all made so much sense. I wouldn't miss reading my Bible every day now. I never imagined it could change me so much. Now, when we sing the hymns in church that used to seem so funny, I think to myself, "That's me! Yes, I know what it means now. That's how it happens to me."'

God wants us to be children no longer, carried by the waves and blown about by every shifting wind of the teaching of deceitful men who lead others into error by the tricks they invent. Instead, we must grow up in every way to Christ (Eph. 4: 14, 15).

Because the Bible is God's book, he never ceases to speak through it. As long as we live we can continue to find fresh truth in its pages. We never know it all. Through the Holy Spirit God always has something more to teach us. 'Let us go forward, then, to mature teaching and leave behind us the first lessons of the Christian message' (Heb. 6: 1).

# CHAPTER 5 –TALKING TO FATHER

Little Boy kneels at the foot of the bed,
Droops on the little hands little gold head.
Hush! Hush! Whisper who dares!
Christopher Robin is saying his prayers.

'God bless Mummy.' I know that's right.
Wasn't it fun in the bath to-night?
The cold's so cold, and the hot's so hot.
Oh! 'God bless Daddy' – I quite forgot.

If I open my fingers a little bit more,
I can see Nanny's dressing-gown on the door.
It's a beautiful blue, but it hasn't a hood.
Oh! 'God bless Nanny and make her good.'

Mine has a hood, and I lie in bed,
And pull the hood right over my head,
And I shut my eyes, and I curl up small,
And nobody knows that I'm there at all.

Oh! 'Thank you, God, for a lovely day.'
And what was the other I had to say?
I said 'Bless Daddy,' so what can it be?
Oh! Now I remember it. 'God bless Me.' (A.A. Milne)

Besides listening to Father, Christians should also want to
talk to him. This is their great privilege. God is not distant
and remote. He is loving and gracious and close at hand.
'God sent the Spirit of his Son into our hearts, the Spirit who

cries out, "Father, my Father"' (Gal. 4: 6). Christians can talk to God as easily and naturally as a little child talks to his parents.

Yet for many Christians, talking to God like this is rarely achieved. All too often their prayers are like Christopher Robin's. They pray briefly at the end of the day when they are desperately tired and ready only for sleep. Somehow they feel that their physical attitude (hands together and eyes closed) is more important than the actual activity in which they are engaged. Their thoughts wander and concentration eludes them. Often they only bring a vague shopping-list of selfish requests to God ('God bless Mummy, God bless Daddy, God bless Nanny, God bless me') and then wonder why their prayers go unanswered. Christopher Robin was middle class and well mannered, so he put himself at the end of the list. Bill came from blunt, northern, working-class stock and was even more selfish. 'God bless me and my wife,' he prayed one day, 'our Joe and his wife, us four and no more. Amen!'

'Lord, teach us to pray,' one of Jesus's disciples asked him (Luke 11: 1). How can we learn to pray as we should, and as we want to? How can prayer become as easy and natural as the conversation between a child and his father?

*Spending time with God*

One day, Jesus went to visit Martha and Mary, two of his closest friends. They were so thrilled he had gone and gladly welcomed him into their home. Martha was determined to lay on a good meal and make sure that Jesus's every need was met. As she fussed and fretted over all the household chores she had set herself, she became more and more exasperated with Mary, her sister, who just sat with Jesus, listening and talking with him. In the end, Martha could stand it no longer. She stormed into the room and, in a vain attempt to be polite, rounded on Mary through Jesus. 'Lord, don't you care that my sister has left me to do all the work by

50

myself?' she exploded. 'Tell her to come and help me!' (Luke 10: 40)

To Martha's surprise, Jesus ignored her request. 'Martha, Martha!' he replied, calmly. 'You are worried and troubled over so many things, but just one is needed. Mary has chosen the right thing, and it will not be taken away from her' (Luke 10: 42).

Interestingly, Luke tells this story just before he outlines Jesus's teaching on prayer. We only learn to pray properly when, like Mary, we learn to spend time with Jesus. As we shall see, we can pray anywhere at any time, but we only learn that art when we have learned to practise regular prayer first.

Wise fathers learn to make time to spend with their children. God always has time for us, so we must learn to make time to spend with him. Older generations of Christians always urged new Christians to set aside a regular time each day for Bible reading and prayer. First thing in the morning was the period recommended for this daily 'Quiet Time'. It was good advice and we would recommend it too. For many people, first thing in the morning is the only time they can pray without being disturbed. Prayer sets the tone for the day and makes it easy for us to walk with God during our remaining, waking hours. For some, early morning is the best time when they can think clearly and concentrate on their conversation with God.

But for others, early morning is totally impractical for a regular Quiet Time. Whatever they do, they must not feel guilty about this, but find another time instead when they can talk to God. Mothers with babies and small children may find it better to set aside time for God just after breakfast or lunch. Commuters, with long, morning train journeys, may find fifteen minutes in a church during their lunch hour is their best time to be regularly quiet. George, who worked on a farm, learned to pray regularly during the time when he had connected the cows to the milking machine. He had to rise at five as it was, and rising any earlier was totally unreasonable.

51

So find the best time for yourself. Make it regular and be disciplined about it. Real prayer only begins when, like Mary, we spend time with Jesus and enjoy doing it.

## Praying for the right things

'I used to believe in God,' confided Jacqui one day, 'and then my aunt became very ill. I prayed that God would make her well again. But she died, so now I don't believe in God any more.'

Jacqui's prayer was natural. Anyone wants to see a sick person healed, and can quite properly pray to God for that end. But Jacqui failed to realise that prayer is more than coming to God with demanding requests in times of crisis, expecting him to answer as we think he should. Prayer involves knowing the will of God and praying according to his will. 'The Father will give you whatever you ask of him *in my name*,' said Jesus (John 15: 16). Many prayers are not offered in Jesus's name, so it is hardly surprising if they go unanswered.

When one of Jesus's disciples asked him to teach them to pray, Luke tells us how he replied. 'Jesus said to them, "When you pray, say this:

'Father:

> May your holy name be honoured;
> may your Kingdom come.
> Give us day by day the food we need.
> Forgive us our sins,
>     for we forgive everyone who does us wrong.
> And do not bring us to hard testing'"' (Luke 11: 2-4).

According to Jesus, the honour of our Father's name and the coming of his Kingdom are far more important than our own needs and desires. Around the world God's name is not honoured, yet it is his world. He made it and he controls it. How often do we pray for the honour of God's name?

52

In the world, God is building his Kingdom in the lives of those who submit to the Lordship of Jesus. How often do we pray for the extension and strengthening of that Kingdom? How much do we pray for evangelism and the growth of God's church at home and abroad? These are the things Jesus tells us to pray for. We cannot complain when our other prayers go unanswered, if we are not praying as Jesus said we should.

Only when we have prayed for the honour of God's name and the coming of his Kingdom can we pray for ourselves. Even then, our prayers are to be strictly limited.

First, we may pray for the satisfaction of our basic daily needs. Sufficient food and clothing are all we need, together with a roof over our heads, and materially that is all we pray for. When David was nine his best friend possessed an electric train set. David wanted one himself more than anything else. So one December, David began to pray for an electric train set for Christmas. Yet despite the fact he let his parents know how he was praying his prayer went unanswered. For it was the wrong prayer. Although his parents had little money they always kept him clothed and fed, and over the years David had to learn to be grateful for that.

Secondly, we must pray for forgiveness. This is our constant spiritual need. For although all our sins are forgiven at the cross of Jesus, and although as Christians we have received God's new life, we still continue to do wrong. God only makes us like Jesus little by little. The process is sometimes painful and slow. Like Paul, we do not do the good we want to; instead, we do the evil we do not want to do (Rom. 7: 19). And so we need to come to the cross again and again, in our prayers, to ask for our Father's forgiveness.

Thirdly, we must pray for right attitudes towards others. Jesus teaches us to say, 'we forgive everyone who does us wrong'. Do we? Thousands of Christians lose the joy of their Father's forgiveness because they bear resentments and grudges against others. They allow their dislike of others to fester in their hearts instead of praying for them. They become judgmental of others and self-righteous in their attitude to themselves. But time and again Jesus and the New Testament writers tell us to love one another, and our enemies too. How we need to pray for right attitudes to the behaviour and personalities of others!

Fourthly, we must pray for strength in temptation. 'Your enemy, the Devil, roams round like a roaring lion, looking for someone to devour' (1 Pet. 5: 8). Against his evil tricks and his burning arrows we need all the armour that God supplies (Eph. 6: 10-20). But God keeps his promise. He does not allow us to be tested beyond our power to remain firm. At the time we are put to the test he gives the strength to endure it, and so provides a way out (1 Cor. 10: 13). So, in praying for ourselves, we should pray for protection from temptation.

## Keeping on praying

When Jesus had taught his disciples the *Lord's Prayer*, he told them the outrageous story of the man who woke his neighbour at midnight to borrow food for an unexpected friend who had arrived from a long journey. Naturally the neighbour was angry, and reluctant to comply with the request. But in the end he got up and gave the man everything he needed because he was not ashamed to keep on asking (Luke 11: 8).

So often, our prayers go unanswered because we give up too easily. Once again our image of God is of a benevolent Father Christmas figure in the sky waiting to grant our every request. And the moment he fails to respond we lose heart and do not ask him any more.

But God is a loving Father, who understands that we, his selfish children, should not always have everything we want instantaneously. Children need to learn patience, and so do we. Children need discipline, so God disciplines us for our good, so that we may share his holiness (Heb. 12: 10).

Even when we are asking for the right things in the right

way, God's timescale is not always the same as ours, and so we need to persist in our prayers. Graham faced a dilemma. Julie and her boyfriend had come and asked him, as a minister, to marry them. Only there was a problem. Julie was a Christian while her boyfriend was not. To make matters worse, Julie was already expecting the boyfriend's child. Several other ministers in her denomination had refused Julie's request and, in desperation, she had finally approached Graham.

Graham agreed to meet Julie's boy. He seemed a sincere lad, anxious to do his best for Julie in the situation for which he was responsible. He was not a Christian but was in no way hostile to Julie's faith, nor to allowing her to practise it after their marriage. So Graham conducted the wedding and Julie was duly married.

From that day forward Graham and his wife began to pray for Julie's husband. Every day they prayed that God would bring him to a living faith in Jesus Christ. For month after month, and year after year, they continued to pray until finally, after fifteen years, their prayers were answered and Julie's husband became a Christian. How willing are we to pray for fifteen years for God to answer our prayers? Jesus says, 'Everyone who asks will receive, and he who seeks will find, and the door will be opened to anyone who knocks' (Luke 11: 10).


*Praying in the Holy Spirit*


At the end of his guidelines for prayer in Luke 11, Jesus compared earthly fathers, who are bad, with the Father in heaven, who is altogether good. 'Would any of you who are fathers give your son a snake when he asks for fish?' Jesus asked. 'Or would you give him a scorpion when he asks for an egg? Bad as you are, you know how to give good things to your children. How much more, then, will the Father in heaven give the Holy Spirit to those who ask him!' (Luke 11: 11-13)

If we are ever going to pray properly, joyously and effectively, we are going to need the Holy Spirit. Without the Holy Spirit prayer will be little more than a dull routine and an onerous duty. With the Spirit we shall pray as we should for 'God sent the Spirit of his Son into our hearts, the Spirit who cries out, "Father, my Father"' (Gal. 4: 6). Jesus says that when we pray the Father in heaven will give the Holy Spirit to those who ask him.

We need the Holy Spirit when we pray because we do not know how we ought to pray. Without the Spirit we pray like Christopher Robin, vague, selfish prayers, constantly interrupted by wandering thoughts. But the Spirit comes to help us. He pleads with God for us, and he prays in accordance with God's will. He makes his deepest feelings known in ways which words cannot express (Rom. 8: 26-7).

Not only does the Spirit pray for us from the outside, as it were. Because God has sent him into our hearts, the Spirit prays for us from the inside. He takes our thoughts, he takes our words, he takes our deepest feelings and he forms them into prayer in accordance with God's will. So when we pray in the Spirit, we ourselves are not praying. The Holy Spirit is praying in us, with us and through us.

At one level the Holy Spirit prays through our natural thoughts and words. He guides and controls what we think and say. But in the New Testament we find the Holy Spirit praying at a different level as well. When the disciples of Jesus were filled with the Holy Spirit on the Day of Pentecost they 'began to talk in other languages, as the Spirit enabled them to speak' (Acts 2: 4). In the same way, Cornelius, his relatives and friends, spoke in tongues and praised God's greatness when the Holy Spirit came down on them (Acts 10: 44-6; 11: 15-17). Similarly, twelve men at Ephesus spoke in tongues and proclaimed God's greatness when the Holy Spirit came upon them (Acts 19: 6).

Paul says that the one who speaks in tongues speaks to God; he speaks secret truths by the power of the Spirit. He helps, or edifies, or builds up himself. No wonder Paul says, 'I would like all of you to speak in ... tongues ... For if I pray in this way, my spirit prays ... I will pray with my spirit, but I will pray also with my mind' (1 Cor. 14: 1-5, 14, 15).

For hundreds of years this level of prayer in the Spirit was largely lost in the strong, mainline churches of Western Christendom. Around the turn of the present century it was rediscovered by thousands of Christians around the world. In time they came to form Pentecostal churches; their growth and influence in the Americas and Asia has been rapid and profound. The last twenty years have seen another wave of discovery among Christians world-wide. Thousands of Christians of every denominational persuasion have found their prayer lives transformed, their devotion deepened, their inner wounds healed and their witness enhanced as they have learned to pray, in the Spirit, in other languages. Sometimes, as on the Day of Pentecost, the languages have been other human languages and have been recognised as such. At other times Christians have prayed in languages of angels (1 Cor. 13: 1). Either way, the Spirit has been praying and blessing has followed.

For obvious reasons, many Christians remain hesitant about this level of Spirit-directed prayer. Mistranslations of the Greek word *glossolalia* in some modern versions of the Bible have not helped. The word simply means 'other languages'. There are no emotional overtones as *The New English Bible*'s 'tongues of ecstasy' suggests. There is nothing harmful or mysterious involved as the *Good News Bible*'s 'strange tongues' infers. When a Christian prays in tongues he is simply praying in another language. He remains in full control of his faculties and his senses, just as he does when he is praying naturally.

Unfortunately, as in the New Testament church at Corinth, some Christians have overrated speaking in tongues. They have forced it insensitively on others. They have tried to divide Christians into first-class and second-class children of God according to whether or not they pray in this way. Wild scenes of excess have sometimes characterised their meetings where the gift has been publicly

57

exercised. But the answer to abuse is not disuse but right use. Praying in tongues was natural and accepted in the first-century church. Many early Christians believed that Jesus had linked the gift with the Great Commission to go into all the world to preach the Gospel to all mankind (Mark 16: 15-18). Whenever God's Spirit has renewed and revived his church, praying in tongues has almost always been rediscovered.

Some Christians learn to pray in tongues as easily and naturally as a growing child learns to talk. One of Gillian's children was displaying disturbing behaviour patterns. No amount of corrective discipline seemed to help. During a visit to discuss the problem, Gillian's pastor suggested she should pray over her child while he was asleep. A few days later she tried to take her pastor's advice, but as she stood in the darkened bedroom her prayers hit a blank wall. 'Lord, teach me to pray,' Gillian cried. 'Pray in tongues,' came the reply, and she did.

Others need help from others. For years, Jenny had longed for the gift and had often asked for it in her private times of prayer. But when nothing ever happened she ruefully concluded the gift was not for her. Finally, in desperation, Jenny visited another Christian with the special gift of helping others to pray in tongues. The friend prayed for Jenny, she laid her hands on her and asked that God would fill her with his Spirit. Then, as she prayed in tongues herself, she encouraged Jenny to join in. Stumblingly and falteringly at first, and then with growing confidence the words came until Jenny was praying as fluently and naturally as she could ordinarily speak in her native language.

The gift of the Holy Spirit in prayer is a good gift. It cannot be anything else. 'Bad as you are,' said Jesus, 'you know how to give good things to your children. How much more, then, will the Father in heaven give the Holy Spirit to those who ask him!' (Luke 11: 13).

If you want to pray in the Spirit in another language, then

ask God for the gift. 'Ask,' said Jesus, 'and you will receive ... For everyone who asks will receive' (Luke 11: 9, 10). Then open your mouth and let sounds come out. Try not to listen to the sounds; that will only inhibit you and put you off. Do not worry if the sounds seem repetitive. Babies only learn one or two words when they begin to talk; they add to their stock of words gradually. Make a point of praying in your new language every day. With practice, it will become easier and more fluent. If you are tempted to think that all you are doing is making up gobbledegook, find another Christian who also prays in this way and pray with him or her in your tongue for a while. You may both pray together, and in this situation there is no need for an interpretation. By praying in your languages together you will encourage one another to know that the Spirit is really praying through you, and that what you are doing is not some human nonsense.

As you learn to pray in the Spirit, you will discover you can use your gift anywhere and at any time. When you are driving the car, pushing the pram and exercising the dog, you can use your new language to the glory of God. We may never understand Paul's command to pray without ceasing until we learned to pray in tongues. It seemed an impossible demand. We are still far from perfect, but we are beginning to learn the secret of constant prayer. For Paul also says, 'Pray at all times in the Spirit' (Eph. 6: 18 RSV); what can he mean except this level of prayer in another language?

As you learn to pray in the Spirit you will also find your whole Christian life will be transformed. However good it was before, it will be that much better. As Jackie Pullinger began to pray in tongues in Hong Kong she discovered that people were being converted through her witness. She could not understand why until she realised that now God was bringing her way those he had prepared to receive Jesus (Jackie Pullinger, *Chasing the Dragon*). Besides the power to witness, the Bible will come alive, Christian worship will be real and growth in grace and the fruits of the Spirit will take place. 'Until now you have not asked for anything in my name,' said Jesus; 'ask and you will receive, so that your happiness may be complete' (John 16: 24).

# CHAPTER 6 –LIKE FATHER, LIKE SON

Mum parks the push-chair outside the supermarket. She transfers little Brian to that useful compartment on the front of the shopping trolley, but before she can move five yards, she is surrounded by admiring friends.

'He *is* growing up! Not a baby now! No one could wonder whether he's a boy or girl any more!'

'Yes, but who does he *look* like?'

'Why, his mother of course! Those *eyes*!'

'No – his *dad*! See the way his mouth goes up one side when he laughs. And that *hair*!'

So the discussion continues. A few years older, the hapless little boy finds it boring and embarrassing. Standing there, twisting his scarf in his hands, he learns to his horror that he possesses his brother's ears, his father's temper and his sister's way of walking (his *sister's*!).

'I'm not bits of someone else. I'm *me*!' he wants to say, ungrammatically but justifiably. Yet the neighbours and friends are correct too. They expect to see the family likeness repeating itself and family traits reappearing. Scientific discovery assures us that they will and must. The genetic bank has a very large but nevertheless limited number of variations. Little Brian from chapter 4 soon discovered that his early passion for reading was a replica of that which consumed his father and his father before him, though both of them were self-taught. So was a nose that resolutely refused to grow at the right angles to his face, and a way of walking sometimes unkindly described as a cross between Charlie Chaplin and a penguin! Then developed their love of arguments and their unconscious bent towards leadership.

One of Brian's own sons in turn developed every one of the same characteristics. He found it uncanny to look at his son on one side and his father on the other. But this is Nature's way. Life reproduces in its own image.

This is God's way, too. Why has God brought millions of children, by new birth, into his family? The staggering answer is twofold; to make us like the Father, and to reproduce replicas in glorious variety of the Son.

## The Father wants us to be like him

When God made human beings he made them like himself (Gen. 1: 26, 27). This was what made them different from the rest of creation; they resembled him. Then they rebelled, and the resemblance of God in human life was marred. But God's purpose is to restore that divine likeness. He began in the Old Testament through the Jews, and he continues in the New Testament through Christ.

'He is going to make good his words...He will make the feeblest and filthiest of us into a god or goddess, a dazzling, radiant, immortal creature, pulsating all through with such energy and joy and wisdom and love as we cannot now imagine...The process will be long and in parts very painful; but that is what we are in for. Nothing less' (C.S. Lewis).

'You must be holy, because I am holy,' is God's insistent command, in the Old Testament and in the New (Lev. 11: 44, 45; 19: 2; 1 Pet. 1: 16). The family likeness that was lost will be restored.

## The Father wants us to be like our elder brother

Because God lives in light that no one can approach, because no one has ever seen him or ever can (1 Tim. 6: 16), we cannot really know how we should be like him. So God has sent us his Son. In him he has shown us what he is like. In his Son, God has given us a standard to live by and an example

62

to follow. Until we meet him ourselves, he wants us to be like Jesus. 'Those whom God had already chosen', says Paul, 'he also set apart to become like his Son, so that the Son would be the first among many brothers' (Rom. 8: 29).

## The Father wants us to be set apart for him

The idea of holiness comes strangely to modern ears. It suggests stern piety, sombre religiosity, a negative attitude to life, monks and nuns, and disapproving Victorians in black suits. In fact holiness is not like this at all. In the Bible, things and people are holy when they are set apart for God. So the Sabbath is a holy day, because it is set apart by God for rest and worship. The Temple is a holy building, because it is set apart for the worship and service of God. Furniture and utensils used in the Temple are holy, because they are not to be used for any other purpose than that laid down. People, similarly, become holy when they are set apart for God.

'My life's my own! I'll do with it as I please!' is the normal human attitude to life. But we are not our own. We were made by a loving Father who, as our creator, retains his rights over us. As God's children, we were bought with a price, the price of Christ's blood poured out for us on the cross.

Holiness begins when we recognise that God has set us apart to become like his Son. Holiness continues when we set ourselves apart, actively co-operating with him in becoming like Jesus. Holiness starts with the surrender of our wills to God. We belong to him. Our lives are his, so he must direct their course. Where we should work, how we should live, whom we should marry; these and all the everyday decisions of life should now be made with reference to him. If this seems hard, we should remember that this was what Jesus did. Once when his disciples were begging him to have some food, he said, 'My food is to obey the will of the one who sent me' (John 4: 34). At the end of his life as he faced the cross he prayed, 'Remove this cup [of suffering] from me; yet not what I will, but what thou wilt' (Mark 14: 36 RSV). When we give our wills with their decision-making powers back to God, then we shall begin to be holy and set apart for him.

Have we then no rights – the right to a settled home, to a steady job, to marry and raise a family? Many of us will indeed continue to enjoy these things for God will give them back to us. But when we are set apart for God he may require us to give up some things which everyone else takes for granted. John and Pauline lived in twelve different homes in seven years because God kept moving them around. Some of their friends gave up a steady job with good prospects and a guaranteed pension to sell Christan literature for a song in East Africa. Another said 'No' to three different men who asked her to marry them, not because they were unsuitable, nor because she was not attracted to them, but because they did not share her call to spend their lives as she knew God wanted her to spend hers.

God wants us to become like Jesus, and he had no rights. He gave up all he had and went to the cross to bring us into the family of his Father. After he was baptised he had nowhere to lie down and rest (Matt. 8: 20). He gave up his job of work, with all the dignity that brought, and lived off the charitable gifts of women (Luke 8: 3). He never married, though he obviously enjoyed the company of women, and they in turn found him deeply attractive. And at the end of his life, Jesus gave up the right to a fair trial and the right to execute vengeance on his enemies as he went willingly to the cross for our salvation. Paul says, 'The attitude you should have is the one that Christ Jesus had ... ' (Phil. 2: 5). Peter says, 'Christ himself suffered for you and left you an example, so that you would follow in his steps' (1 Pet. 2: 21).

*The Father wants us to turn our backs on the past*

Before we are born into God's family, the Bible says we live

64

'in the flesh'. It means that we live in bodies with characters that are spoiled by our rebellion against God. As such we live to please ourselves. Often, in various ways, we wander into evil and into direct disobedience to God's rules for our lives. To become like Jesus we are required to turn our backs on all that.

Time and again in his letters Paul lists aspects of human behaviour which belong to the old life 'in the flesh'. 'Get rid of them,' he says. 'Don't behave like this any more.'

Sexual immorality was often top of Paul's lists (Gal. 5: 19; Col. 3: 5). His world was as immoral as ours, probably more so. Many of his converts came to Christ with sullied pasts. Freely forgiven in Jesus they were to turn away from this kind of behaviour. Christians should not sleep around, nor should they sleep together before they marry, nor should they have affairs after they marry. In God's book, sex is for marriage, and that is where it should be for the Christian.

Dishonesty is another of Paul's 'don'ts'. 'Do not lie to one another,' he says (Col. 3: 9). 'The man who used to rob must stop robbing and start working' (Eph. 4: 28). Not only open theft and deceit are forbidden to the Christian, but their subtler forms as well. Tax evasion, scrounging, idling at work and from work, 'white lies' are all forms of deceit from which the Christian must turn away. They are part of the past, part of the 'old life' lived out of sorts with God.

Idolatry always features among Paul's lists of behaviour which characterise the old life. The Greek culture in which he lived was openly pagan with temples to every god and goddess on every street corner. Associated with their worship were degrading and perverted acts which eventually bound and enslaved those who practised them. Today idolatry is making a comeback with the revival of occult practices, magic and Satanism. Any Christian who has had any contact with any of these before his birth into the family of God must renounce them in the Name of Jesus and have nothing to do with them ever again. If the evil powers behind them have bound him then he must seek deliverance in Jesus's name.

The worship of false gods can also take subtler forms. 'Greed is a form of idolatry,' Paul says (Col. 3: 5), and immediately he touches one of the commonest sins of the modern world. The desire to have more and more, at any price, is a form of idolatry. The belief that things in themselves bring satisfaction is one of the deceits of idolatry. Anything which becomes the driving force of my life, other than Jesus, is an idol. Whatever I have lived for, advancement in my profession, the accumulation of wealth, power over others, pre-eminence in sport, an annual holiday, a hobby, a home, must now take second place to Jesus.

Bad language in all its forms is something else from which we must turn away. 'No insults or obscene talk must ever come from your lips' (Col. 3: 8). 'If you become angry, do not let your anger lead you into sin, and do not stay angry all day' (Eph. 4: 26). No more shouting then, no more use of God's Name in vain. Like other forms of evil, this also belongs to 'the flesh'.

Drunkenness is something else from which the Christian must turn. Nowhere does the Bible condemn the drinking of alcoholic liquor as such; some times it recommends it (1 Tim. 5: 23). Nowhere does the Bible command total abstinence from alcohol, though some people who took vows of dedication did abstain and were commended (Num. 6: 1-4; Judg. 13: 2-7; Luke 1: 15). But drunkenness is always forbidden. 'Do not get drunk with wine, which will only ruin you;' says Paul; 'instead be filled with the Spirit' (Eph. 5: 18).

Hardest of all, the Christian is called to deal with evil thoughts. Jesus said, 'From the inside, from a person's heart, come the evil ideas which lead him to do immoral things, to rob, kill, commit adultery, be greedy and do all sorts of evil things; deceit, indecency, jealousy, slander, pride and folly' (Mark 7: 21). Our thoughts control our actions, so unless we learn to think right we shall never be set apart for God. 'We take every thought captive,' says Paul, 'and make it obey Christ' (2 Cor. 10: 5). So we are told to get rid of bitterness, passion and anger. We must have no more hateful feelings of any sort. Grudges, resentment and smouldering determination to get even with those who have wronged us are all part of the way of the world, all part of the thought-life of those who live 'in the flesh'. And they yield a bitter harvest. Hypertension, heart disease, stomach ulcers, insomnia and premature ageing can be traced, again and again, to hurtful thoughts, harboured and nurtured by those who have never known the forgiving love of Christ. For the Christian they are wrong, and he must put them away.

*The Father wants our lives to be transformed*

Holiness is never simply a list of 'don'ts'. Christians have sometimes given this impression when they have concentrated too much on the negative aspects of their life in Jesus. Sometimes they have become harsh and judgmental towards others, and have given the false impression that the Christian life is deadly serious and devoid of fun and joy. Nothing could be further from the truth.

Jesus himself was full of fun and laughter. Many of his stories were uproariously funny when he first told them. Only in translation have they lost their subtle irony and humour. Jesus made fun of his friends and gave them nicknames which aptly described the idiosyncrasies of their characters (Mark 3: 17; John 1: 42, 47). He liked good food and wine, and the company of doubtful characters (Luke 7: 34). He allowed disreputable women to smother him in public with embarrassing displays of affection (Mark 14: 3-5, Luke 7: 37, 38; John 12: 1-6). Yet he never sinned. Jesus never crossed the line betweem enjoying life to the full and doing wrong. And he came that we might too enjoy life in all its fullness (John 10: 10).

For every thing the Christian must not do, there is something else he must do in its place. 'Do not conform yourselves to the standards of this world,' says Paul, 'but let God trasform you inwardly by a complete change of your mind' (Rom. 12: 2). When our minds are changed, our behaviour will change. When our thoughts are transformed we shall know God's will, for we shall think as he does. Our behaviour, in turn, will be good, pleasing to God and perfect (Rom. 12: 2).

Abandoning hurtful feelings, we shall become kind, tender-hearted and forgiving (Eph. 4: 32). Where anger and passion dominated our thoughts we shall instead be clothed with compassion, kindness, humility, gentleness and patience. Where we failed to suffer fools gladly we shall become tolerant of the foibles and failures of others. Sacrificial, self-giving love will become the hallmark of our lives. Where we were full of suspicion and anxiety, the peace that Christ gives will govern our minds and guide us in the decisions we make. Where once we grumbled when anyone or anything did not suit us, we shall learn to thank God for his goodness and praise him in every situation life brings (Col. 3: 12-17).

If drunkenness once controlled our lives, leading us into all kinds of folly and harmful behaviour, God now wants us to be filled and controlled with his Spirit. If bad language characterised our conversation, our speech now should always be pleasant and interesting (Col. 4: 6). If greed consumed us and dishonesty was part of our stock-in-trade we should 'start working, in order to earn an honest living ...and to be able to help the poor' (Eph. 4: 28).

Indeed, the Christian's attitude to money is one of the surest marks of his holiness. His money is no longer his own, to spend as he pleases. It comes from God, and God has first claim on its use. Paul constantly urges his readers to give generously to meet the needs of others. He commends the Macedonians who 'gave as much as they could, and even more than they could' (2 Cor. 8: 3). He reminds his readers of Christ, who, 'rich as he was...made himself poor for your sake, in order to make you rich by means of his poverty' (2 Cor. 8: 9).

Jews in the Old Testament were required to give at least a tenth of their produce to Temple and synagogue funds for the support of the priesthood, maintenance of the fabric and the relief of the poor. Similarly, a tenth of one's income is the absolute minimum the Christian should give to the support of the church at home and overseas and the needs of worthwhile charitable causes. Through covenanting, Christians who pay income tax can increase this money by nearly half as much again.

Our gift to God's work should not come last on our spending list, but first. We should not give grudgingly, but cheerfully (2 Cor. 9: 7). We should not give ostentatiously, but secretly, as far as we are able (Matt. 6: 2-4). We should not give occasionally but regularly and prayerfully.

When we give in this way God promises to overturn the normal economic rules which govern the handling of money and the acquisition of wealth. Normally, the less we spend the more we make, the more we look after ourselves the richer we become. But God says that when we put him first, when we give our money first to him, to his church and to the needs of his world, he will more than make up to us what we have given. And he calls us to believe what he says and act accordingly.

'Bring the full amount of your tithes to the Temple,' he said to the Jews. Don't scrape and skimp, and keep as much back as you can for yourself. 'Put me to the test and you will see that I will open the windows of heaven and pour out on you in abundance all kinds of good things' (Mal. 3: 10). 'God, who supplies seed to sow and bread to eat.' Paul says in the New Testament, 'will also supply you with all the seed you need and will make it grow and produce a rich harvest from your generosity' (2 Cor. 9: 10).

This does not mean that the more we give the richer we shall become financially, for then all Christians would be millionaires. But it does mean that when we give God the first of our money, as he commands, we shall always have enough for ourselves and some more left over to give again (2 Cor. 9: 8-11). And although we may be relatively poor in comparison with our friends and neighbours, we shall become rich towards God through our generosity. 'Store up riches for yourselves in heaven' says Jesus. 'For your heart will always be where your riches are' (Matt. 6: 20, 21).

Not only in the way they spend their money, but also in the way they spend their time Christians are called to be different. For as their money belongs to God, so does their time. 'Look carefully then how you walk,' says Paul, '... making the most of the time, because the days are evil' (Eph. 5: 16 RSV). So Christians should not live for time to please themselves, as others do. Of course they need time to relax, to enjoy themselves, to pursue personal interests and hobbies; this is after all the Father's world. But above all else the Christian's time should be spent in learning and obeying the will of God, in serving and relieving the needs of others. Time for Bible reading and prayer, time for worship and service; these should be the Christian's priorities and not his annual holiday or his trip into the country next weekend.

Especially in his use of Sunday the Christian is called to be different from his friends and neighbours around him. From the beginning of time itself God set aside one day in seven as a day of rest. It reflects God's own rest from his creative activity when that work was done. So the Christian who rests on the Sabbath is behaving like his Father in heaven.

Jesus constantly insisted that 'the Sabbath was made for the good of man; man was not made for the sabbath' (Mark 2: 27). He treated with cavalier disregard many of the Jewish rules about the Sabbath which had made it a miserable and restricting day for many people. He showed that religious rules can be broken to relieve human beings in need (Mark 2: 25-6). By healing the sick on the Sabbath Jesus demonstrated that some work is lawful and proper.

But Jesus also claimed a lordship over the Sabbath himself which angered and infuriated his contemporaries (Mark 2: 28). In his resurrection he invested it with a new significance and meaning. From the very beginning of the church Christians worshipped Jesus on the first day of the week. As soon as social conditions allowed they transferred their Sabbath observance to that day from Saturday, thereby honouring God in his creation and rejoicing in Jesus's mighty resurrection.

How the Christian spends Sunday is therefore an

indication of his obedience and holiness. Worship, at least once in the day and preferably twice, should be a priority. Nothing, not even Sunday School teaching or other Christian service, should normally be allowed to stand in the way of this. Christians who agree to teach children during the Sunday morning service of worship should only do so if they are able and willing to attend worship themselves regularly in the evening.

Christian service (sharing in worship, visiting the sick, caring for the lonely and elderly) is another proper Sunday activity, as long as it does not become too tiring and exhausting in itself. For Sunday is a day of rest, and Christians should not be so tired after Sunday that they cannot work properly on Monday.

Rest from normal work is therefore vital every Sunday. Christians whose employment requires them to work on Sundays may face a crucial test of obedience here. Some Sunday work is obviously right, particularly in the medical and caring professions. Christians here will worship whenever they can and ensure they take a day's rest on another day of the week. But much Sunday work is not necessary, and some Christians may have to face loss of earnings through avoiding Sunday overtime out of obedience to Christ. Others may feel they should change their jobs in order to keep the Christian Sabbath.

Christians should also avoid causing others to work on Sunday. Christian employers should enable their employees to observe Sunday as they would wish to themselves. But other Christians too should try to minimise the amount of Sunday work they cause others. Therefore, they should try to avoid buying and selling on Sunday and should stay away from sporting events on this day. Instead, they should spend their time in wholesome, relaxing activities with their families and friends.

Our great-grandfathers kept the 'holy Sabbath'. Our grandfathers kept the 'Sabbath'. Our fathers observed Sunday, while we enjoy the weekend. So an increasingly secular society has encroached on Sunday, the Christian

Sabbath. In our observance of Sunday we should not be miserable kill-joys, only concerned with what we should not do. But we should be positive and wholesome in our worship of Jesus, who is alive, and in taking rest from our work as God our Father rested from his.

So Christians are called to be different, in the way they think, in the way they behave towards others, in the way they talk, in the way they handle their money, in the way they spend their time, and in their deepest personal relationships. In place of immorality they should practise chastity. In courtship, they should behave with the deepest respect for one another, always trying never to hurt their partner, never to do anything they might later regret if the courtship comes to an end. Love and fidelity should characterise their marriages. 'Husbands, love your wives just as Christ loved the church and gave his life for it.' 'Wives, submit to your husbands as to the Lord' (Eph. 5: 25, 22). Many have found the latter command difficult, but when a man loves his wife as Jesus loves his church, then she should have no difficulty in submitting to him as she should to Christ. Family life, too, should display love, respect, discipline and obedience, in that order (Eph. 6: 1-4).

The road to holiness is hard and long. The more we follow Jesus the more aware we become of our failure and imperfection. Attractive sins continue to dog us and let us down. Attainment of positive graces often seems to recede into the ever-distant future. Deep wounds in our character, inflicted in infancy and childhood, leave scars which can spoil our Christian behaviour for years. This side of heaven we never become completely like Jesus. This side of heaven we keep striving to win the prize for which Christ Jesus has already won us to himself (Phil. 3: 12).

Living a holy life, however, is not a completely impossible task. God does not call us to holiness in order to condemn us on account of our constant failure. Jesus, who by his death brought us into the family in the first place, continues to encourage and strengthen us. When we fail he pleads with the Father on our behalf (1 John 2: 1). So when we confess our sins to God, he forgives us and purifies us from all wrongdoing (1 John 1: 9).

Nor are we left to struggle on our own. If we merely try to be holy all we shall ever become is self-righteous, judgmental hypocrites, unyielding moralists with a bank of secret failures we never dare admit. Jesus constantly assists us in our endeavours. The more we trust in him and not in ourselves the more he makes us like himself. In our struggle against sin we have four great incentives to enable us to overcome.

## 1   We have the power of Christ's love

Love in itself is a redemptive and improving thing. Notice how the behaviour of two people in love improves. Their love for each other brings out the best in themselves. A selfish, wayward youth becomes courteous and kind. A sharp-tongued girl learns to reply softly.

If human love can do this, how much more can the love of Jesus and our response make us better! 'We are ruled by the love of Christ,' says Paul. 'He died for all, so that those who live should no longer live for themselves, but only for him who died and was raised to life for their sake' (2 Cor. 5: 15).

A stiff and starchy dinner-party at the home of Simon the Pharisee was interrupted by a prostitute who lavished tears and extravagant perfume on the feet of Jesus as he reclined at the table. When Simon objected within himself that a prophet would never allow such a woman to touch him, Jesus replied with the story of the moneylender. Two debtors owed him five hundred silver coins and fifty silver coins respectively. When neither could pay he cancelled the debts. 'Which one,' asked Jesus, 'will love him more?'

'The one who was forgiven more,' answered Simon.

'You are right,' said Jesus, and went on to explain how the woman had supplied the common courtesy of foot-washing which Simon had omitted because 'her many sins have been forgiven. But whoever has been forgiven little shows only a little love' (Luke 7: 36-47).

We shall never make much progress in holiness until we fall in love with Jesus. But when we begin to understand the extent of his love, when we see him dying on the cross for *our* sins, when we sob in reply, 'Why me?' then we shall begin to become like him.

## 2 We have the presence of Christ's Spirit

Our improved behaviour when we fall in love often does not last. Our love grows cold and we revert to our former selfish way of life. And from time to time our love for Christ grows cold, although his love for us remains.

So beside his love Christ gives us his Spirit. When we are born into God's family, Christ's Spirit comes to live inside us. He begins to make us like Jesus, for he is the Spirit of Jesus. We do not become holy by trying; 'the Spirit produces love, joy, peace, patience, kindness, goodness, faithfulness, humility and self-control' (Gal. 5: 22). So if we want to be holy we must let the Spirit direct our lives, and then we shall not gratify the desires of the flesh (Gal. 5: 16). As we once surrendered ourselves as slaves to impurity and wickedness, now we must surrender ourselves as slaves of righteousness for holy purposes (Rom. 6: 19).

So we must not grieve the Spirit by putting ourselves in the way of temptation, nor must we quench the Spirit by hanging on to sins from the past. 'Do not get drunk with wine, which will only ruin you; instead be filled with the Spirit' (Eph. 5: 18). 'Go on being filled,' is the force of Paul's words. When you fail, and confess your sin, ask for the fullness of Christ's Spirit again. When your love grows cold, ask Jesus to fill you with his Spirit once more. He always will, for the Father loves to give the Holy Spirit to those who ask him (Luke 11: 13).

## 3 We have the provision of Christ's table

We can never become holy on our own. We need the

fellowship and support of other Christians. They are engaged in the same struggle as ourselves. They are facing the same temptations and striving for the same graces as we are. As we share with them our weaknesses and strengths we mutually encourage one another.

Regular attendance at Christian worship is one of our greatest aids to holiness. There we sing God's praise, there we hear God's word, there we bring our prayers together. 'Observe the Sabbath and keep it holy,' says the fourth commandment (Exod. 20: 8). 'I was in the Spirit on the Lord's day,' wrote the apostle John (Rev. 1: 10 RSV) indicating that the early Christians quickly transferred the observance of the Sabbath from Saturday to Sunday in memory of the resurrection. It we want to be holy, regular involvement in Christian worship on Sunday will become a top priority of our week.

In Christian worship, one service above all others, the Communion Service, encourages us to holiness and produces it. Here we confess our sins to Almighty God and receive his pardon. Here we exchange Christ's peace with each other, and how can we do this if brooding resentment and unreconciled wrongs lie between us? Here, with angels and archangels, and with all the company of heaven, we proclaim God's great and glorious name, for ever praising him for his holiness, power, might and glory. Here, in a way no words can explain (though many have tried) Christ is specially present. As we receive the bread and wine, we feed on him in our hearts by faith with thanksgiving. Here we pray:

'fill us with your grace and heavenly blessing,
nourish us with the body and blood of your Son,
that we may grow into his likeness
and, made one by your Spirit,
become a living temple to your glory' *(The Alternative Service Book 1980*, p.135).

If we would grow in holiness, then we should share in Communion as often as we can.

## 4 We have the promise of Christ's return

In his first letter, the apostle John wrote, 'it is not yet clear what we shall become. But we know that when Christ appears, we shall be like him, because we shall see him as he really is' (1 John 3: 2). Christians believe that human history is moving to a climax, the personal return of Jesus Christ in glory. This will bring his work of salvation to completion. When he comes again, God's perfect creation, now spoiled by mankind's rebellion and sin, will be restored. When he comes, our growth in holiness will finish for 'we shall be like him'.

We do not know when Christ will come. No one knows the day and hour (Matt. 24: 36). His coming will be swift, leaving no one time to respond who has not responded to him already (Matt. 24: 40, 41). He will come like a thief when people are least expecting him (2 Pet. 3: 10). And while his final coming is delayed, he keeps coming for each Christian at the moment of death. When we leave our home in the body, we are at home with the Lord. All of us must appear before Christ, to be judged by him (2 Cor. 5: 8-10).

Therefore we are told to be ready, always looking for Christ's return. If we are going to be like him, we must keep ourselves pure, just as Christ is pure (1 John 3: 3).

In 1940 two men, among millions, were called up to serve in the armed forces during the Second World War. Both were separated from the women they loved. One sent regular letters to the girl he had left behind. When he was shipped overseas he sent small gifts from the ports at which the ship called; some pottery from one, some lace from another. One day, as she was wistfully re-reading the letters and fingering the gifts, the door opened and he was there! As she flung herself into his arms, the letters were scattered, the pottery almost knocked from its stand, the lace trodden underfoot. *He* was there; that was so much better than his gifts!

The second man also wrote home regularly, though he received replies less frequently than the other. One day, he too came home on unexpected leave. The house was empty.

At the hospital where his wife worked they said she was off duty. A neighbour gave him an odd look and directed him to the local club. There he found her, sitting hand-in-hand with another man. He soon found a great deal more, and the judge readily granted a divorce. The bridegroom had returned to find the bride unfaithful.

We may not live to see Christ's final, climactic return, but his coming is no farther away than the end of our earthly lives. How will he find us when he appears? Will he find us immersed in his word and rejoicing in his gifts, or will he find us unfaithful, slack and lazy in our Christian profession, turning again to the sins from which he has redeemed us? 'Everyone who has this hope in Christ keeps himself pure, just as Christ is pure' (1 John 3: 3).

# CHAPTER 7 – THE FAMILY FEUD

When we are born into the family of God we become aware, usually for the first time in our lives, of an implacable foe. He has always been our enemy, although we have probably been largely unconscious of his existence, or the harm he has done us. The Bible calls him Satan, or the Devil. He is the Enemy of God. He works to frustrate the will of God in the world, in the community, in the church and in every individual human life. He is not a ghoulish-looking character with horns and a tail like a toasting-fork, but a spiritual being who has existed since before the creation of the world. He controls a whole army of lesser devils, or demons, and through them he promotes evil, wrongdoing and suffering in the world.

Satan's origin is shrouded in mystery. Jesus said, 'I saw Satan fall like lightning from heaven' (Luke 10: 18). Elsewhere the Bible hints that Satan was one of God's angels. But he led a revolt in heaven and was thrown out with all his supporters (Isa. 14: 12-15). In any event he was present at creation. In the guise of the serpent he tempted Adam and Eve to sin, and the whole of God's creation and humanity became spoiled as a result.

In the eternal plan of God, Satan is granted limited power. Jesus describes him as the 'ruler of this world' (John 12: 31; 14: 30; 16: 11). Paul calls him 'the ruler of the spiritual powers in space, the spirit who now controls the people who disobey God' (Eph. 2: 2). He once boasted to Jesus that all the power and wealth of all the kingdoms of the world had been handed over to him. He could give it to anyone he chose (Luke 4: 6). But his boast was empty, for 'the Supreme

God has power over human kingdoms and ... he can give them to anyone he chooses' (Dan. 4: 17).

Before we are born into God's family we live under Satan's control. He lulls most of us into a false sense of security by causing us to doubt his existence at all. Belief in the Devil? Surely that went out with the Middle Ages! If we have problems with right and wrong, well, we are no worse than anyone else. Why worry? Something or someone else is to blame for our faults anyway. Satan cannot be involved.

But when we become God's children, right and wrong assume a new importance. We see ourselves through new eyes, and only the amazing grace of a forgiving God saves us from despair at the extent of wrong in our lives. Meanwhile, Satan himself becomes our relentless enemy. He 'roams round like a roaring lion, looking for someone to devour' (1 Pet. 5: 8). He disguises himself to look like an angel of light (2 Cor. 11: 14). Whenever we do wrong he accuses us before God and in our consciences and makes us feel despair (Rev. 12: 10). We are caught up in a family feud, for Satan and Jesus are implacably opposed, and the enemy declares war on our souls.


*Satan's methods*

Satan tempts us in the same way he tempted Adam and Eve at the beginning of human history, and in the same way he tempted Jesus after his baptism. First, he casts doubt on God's word. 'Did God really tell you not to eat fruit from any tree in the garden?' he asked Eve incredulously (Gen. 3: 1). 'If you are God's Son ... ' he parried, to Jesus, again and again (Matt. 4; Luke 4).

'The Bible, the word of God?' says Satan to us today. 'Don't be ridiculous! It can't be! It's old fashioned! It's full of mistakes! You can't expect God to speak through a book! There's no such thing as right and wrong either! All that went out with the Ark! Right and wrong are what is right and wrong for me, now, in my situation. What's right at one time may be wrong at another, and vice versa. The Bible tells us what was right and wrong when it was written. We cannot expect it to tell us what is right and wrong today.'

So Satan tempts us to doubt that God has spoken, or persuades us that his commands and demands are totally unreasonable. Fancy, putting people in a fruit garden and then forbidding them to eat any of its fruit! Of course, God had not done that, but Satan suggests it. When Eve told him what God had really said he flatly denied the truth in God's words, for Satan is a liar and the father of lies (John 8: 44). When he cannot cause us to doubt God's word by suggestion and inneundo, then he will contradict it out of hand.

Then Satan tempts us to doubt God's love and wisdom. 'You will not die; God said that, because he knows that when you eat it you will be like God and know what is good and what is bad' (Gen. 3: 5). That is what we want, to supplant God, to know everything he knows, to be masters of our own destiny, to be self-sufficient and to be able to live without him. So Satan tempts us to disregard his warnings, to see them as restrictive instead of liberating, and to disobey him in order to know everything.

In a rather different way, Satan tempted Jesus to doubt God's love and care. 'Throw yourself down from the Temple,' he said. 'Go on. You won't hurt yourself. God's angels will care for you. They won't even let you bang your foot on a stone' (Matt. 4: 6).

But Jesus knew that was no way to prove God's love. Had he jumped he would have shown he doubted God's love. He would not have been trusting God but putting him to the test. So he resisted the temptation and the Devil was defeated.

Satan tempts us by what we see. 'The woman saw how beautiful the tree was ... So she took some of the fruit and ate it' (Gen. 3: 6). 'The Devil took Jesus to a very high mountain and showed him all the kingdoms of the world in all their greatness' (Matt. 4: 8). Because the world is God's world it is very good (Gen. 1: 31). Nothing in it is intrinsically evil or harmful. But Satan tempts us to want what we should not have. When King David saw Bathsheba he fell into sin (2 Sam. 11: 2-5). Jesus said, 'anyone who looks at a woman and wants to possess her is guilty of committing adultery with her in his heart' (Matt. 5: 28).

In today's world Satan tempts us through our eyes, perhaps as never before. Television is in all our homes, and while much of it is trivial and harmless some of it is deliberately designed to arouse wrong desires. Television commercials bombard us with things, good things, useful things, extravagant things, but all things which cost money, and thus they make us selfish and dissatisfied. 'The love of money is a source of all kinds of evil. Some have been so eager to have it that they have wandered away from the faith and have broken their hearts with many sorrows' (1 Tim. 6: 10). And the love of money is usually fostered through what we see with our eyes and want to have.

Satan tempts us through our natural desires. When Eve saw how good the fruit would be to eat, she took it (Gen. 3: 6). When Jesus was hungry in the desert Satan tempted him to turn stones into bread (Matt. 4: 3). In themselves there is nothing wrong with our natural desires. They are given to us by God to preserve life and to ensure the continuation of the human race. But Satan tempts us to abuse and misuse them and, in so doing, to turn away from the God who made us and loves us. And because God's world has been spoiled by human rebellion and sin our natural desires have become warped and twisted and make us easy prey to Satan's attacks. 'What our human nature wants is opposed to what the Spirit wants, and what the Spirit wants is opposed to what our human nature wants. These two are enemies, and ... you cannot do what you want to do' (Gal. 5: 17). Immorality, idolatry and witchcraft; aggression, jealousy, anger and ambition; party spirit, envy and drunkenness; all these and other things result when the Devil tempts us through our natural desires (Gal. 5: 19-21).

Satan tempts us through our minds. When Eve thought how wonderful it would be to become wise she took some of the fruit and ate it (Gen. 3: 6). Satan tempted Jesus with the promise of power and world dominion (Matt. 4: 8). We want these more than anything else; wisdom, power and acclaim. And in our pride we imagine we can gain them by ourselves, we can master our own destiny, we can find satisfaction in exercising power over others.

Eyes, natural desires and pride; these are the means Satan uses to tempt us. And in a world at odds with God they make us easy targets for his attacks. For 'what the sinful self desires, what people see and want, and everything in this world that people are so proud of – none of this comes from the Father; it all comes from the world' (1 John 2: 16).

Satan also tempts us through others. When Eve had eaten some of the fruit she gave some to her husband, and he also ate (Gen. 3: 6). When Peter rebuked Jesus for forecasting his death on the cross, Jesus retorted, 'Get away from me, Satan! You are an obstacle in my way, because these thoughts of yours don't come from God, but from man' (Matt. 16: 23).

Some of our strongest temptations come through our friends. We naturally want to do what others do, to be one of the crowd, to be popular and liked. Sometimes the hardest thing we have to do soon after we become Christians is to explain to our friends why our behaviour has changed. But 'When sinners tempt you ... don't give in' (Prov. 1: 10).

Satan's promises often come true, but never in the way we expect. When Adam and Eve ate the forbidden fruit, they were given understanding – and realised they were naked (Gen. 3: 7). Their greatest joy, their perfect wholesome human bodies, became their greatest shame, 'so they sewed fig leaves together and covered themselves' (Gen. 3: 7). Instead of wisdom, they found fear. Instead of joy, they found blame. Their beautiful relationship became one of dominance, subjection and pain. Fulfilment and dignity became wearisome toil. Alienated from God and himself, man's only certainty in life became death. And the whole of God's creation was soiled as a result (Gen. 3: 14-21).

There is enjoyment in sin, but only for a little while (Heb.

11: 25). Only in God's presence are joy and pleasure for ever (Ps. 16: 11). Satan's temptations still bring shame, fear, despair, remorse and death. He still promises everything and produces nothing.

Satan's attacks are fierce. He 'roams round like a roaring lion, looking for someone to devour' (1 Pet. 5: 8). Satan deceives by clever lies (2 Cor. 11: 3). He comes like an angel of light and disguises his servants as servants of righteousness (2 Cor. 11: 14, 15). He has received permission to test us, but Jesus prays for us, that our faith might not fail (Job 1, 2; Luke 22: 31, 32).

## Satan's defeat

Satan, however, is a defeated foe. He was totally defeated in the life, the death and the resurrection of Jesus. This is why Jesus came, 'to destroy what the Devil had done' (1 John 3: 8).

Jesus defeated Satan in his human life. He was tempted in every way that we are, but did not sin (Heb. 4: 15). In the desert, among the crowds, by the Jewish leaders and in the failure of his closest followers, Jesus was constantly tempted to deny his Father, and to turn from doing his Father's will. But Jesus never faltered. Jesus never failed. 'And now he can help those who are tempted, because he himself was tempted and suffered' (Heb. 2: 18).

Jesus defeated Satan in his death. There it seemed as if Satan triumphed. There the faultless Son of God was hung between two murderers. Even Jesus himself described his arrest as the 'hour ... when the power of darkness rules' (Luke 22: 53). But at the cross, 'Christ stripped the spiritual rulers and authorities of their power; he made a public spectacle of them by leading them as captives in his victory procession' (Col. 2: 15 margin).

Jesus defeated Satan in his mighty resurrection. There he defeated the last enemy which is death (1 Cor. 15: 26). Because he lives, we shall live also. Jesus sits at God's right hand until his enemies are made a footstool under his feet.

Because Satan is defeated, his final downfall is certain. His power now is more limited than ever. Although he may yet gather his forces into one final assault on Jesus and his followers, the outcome of the battle is assured. The Bible's final picture of the Devil shows him being thrown into a lake of fire and sulphur to be tormented day and night for ever (Rev. 20: 10).

*Victory over Satan*

Unfortunately, Satan does not behave as if he is defeated; we still have the practical problem of deflecting his attacks each day. For he is still on the prowl. His attacks are insistent. He still tries to draw us away from Christ and back into our old way of life. How can he win in this daily battle?

Victory over Satan begins at the cross. There, where Jesus dies, Satan was conquered. And only when we come and live at the cross will Satan be conquered in our lives. Christians in heaven are there because they have won the victory over Satan by the blood of the Lamb, and only by his blood shall we be victorious too (Rev. 12: 11). The blood of Jesus purifies us from every sin. We come to the cross at the beginning of our Christian lives for forgiveness, and only as we stay there shall we find strength to resist temptation.

Victory continues through daily trust in Jesus Christ. We must trust Jesus as the truth; what he says goes. Then we must trust the truth of the Christian gospel. As long as we believe that the only way to God is through Christ, that our sins are forgiven at the cross, and that through Jesus we are accounted righteous in God's sight, we shall have victory over Satan.

Paul describes the Christian as a soldier wearing the spiritual armour which God provides. He wears truth like a belt around his waist, the righteousness of Jesus across his chest like a breastplate, and salvation as a helmet over his head. This mighty conviction that in Jesus he has found the truth is the best protection he can have against the Devil's attacks.

Then Satan is defeated as we enter into active service for Jesus. Wear, as your shoes, says Paul, the readiness to announce the Good News of peace (Eph. 6: 15). The best form of defence is attack, yet so many Christians live defeated lives because they will not do anything to make Jesus known. They sit around, simply expecting to be on the receiving end all the time. They want to be passive spectators in services, to have a shoulder to cry on whenever they are feeling low, to be constantly bolstered and supported by other members of their fellowship and church. But ask them to do something for Christ, and they are too busy, or they do not have the ability, or God has not given them the gifts for that particular task, or God is not leading them in that direction. So they remain, passengers on God's train, sleeping partners in the family firm, lazy for Christ and easy prey to the Devil's attacks. Satan always finds work for idle hands, and we shall always find excuses for failing to make Christ known. But when we determine to tell others about him, in a certain way, at a certain time, in company with others, then that in itself becomes a powerful antidote to temptation.

When we serve Christ our confidence in him grows. Aware of our weakness we have to trust him to make us strong. And he always does. God's word does not return to him empty. He always honours what we do in Christ's name. Encouraged by the power and reality of Christ, at work in the lives of others, we too are strengthened in our fight against temptation. 'Carry faith as a shield;' says Paul, 'for with it you will be able to put out all the burning arrows shot by the Evil One' (Eph. 6: 16).

We also overcome temptation as we accept and use God's word. God's word, says Paul, is 'the sword which the Spirit gives you' (Eph. 6: 17). Knowledge and use of the Bible was integral of Jesus's victory over Satan. Every time he was tempted in the desert he overcame the temptation with words from the Bible.

'Order these stones to turn into bread,' said the Devil.

But Jesus answered, 'The scripture says, "Man cannot live on bread alone."'

'Throw yourself down,' said the Devil.

Jesus answered, 'The scripture says, "Do not put the Lord your God to the test."'

'All this I will give you,' the Devil said, 'if you kneel down and worship me.'

Then Jesus answered, 'Go away, Satan! The scripture says, "Worship the Lord your God and serve only him!"' (Matt. 4: 1-10).

Had Jesus not known the teaching of the Bible how would he have fought in his contest with Satan? Like Timothy, we should do our best to win God's full approval as workers who are not ashamed because we know how to teach correctly the message of God's truth (2 Tim. 2: 15).

Then we learn to overcome temptation as we learn to pray. Having described every article of armour which the Christian should take to defeat the enemy, Paul adds, 'Do all this in prayer, asking for God's help' (Eph. 6: 18). God's help is what we need in the family feud. Of ourselves we shall always fail, but he is able to keep us and protect us and give us the victory through our Lord Jesus Christ. And only as we pray can we know God's help.

If knowledge of the Bible was one secret of Jesus's victory, prayer was the other. Luke paints a canvas of Jesus engaged in ceaseless activity. Thronged by crowds, waylaid by the sick and those in need of healing, preaching in the synagogues, challenged by demons, Jesus was in constant demand. 'But he would go away to lonely places, where he prayed' (Luke 5: 16). That was the source of Jesus's strength, and his power over all the forces of Satan.

Most of all Jesus prayed as he approached the cross. There his last and greatest battle with the Devil was fought. And before the battle he prayed in Gethsemane for victory. As he prayed an angel from heaven appeared to him and strengthened him. When his disciples slept he warned them to pray that they too would not fall into temptation (Luke 22: 41-6).

Often we are tempted we imagine that our struggle is special to ourselves. No one else is tempted as we are. In fact the opposite is true. 'Every test that you have experienced,' says Paul, 'is the kind that normally comes to people.' Our temptations are not different from others'; they are the same. And God keeps his promise. He does not allow us to be tested beyond our power to remain firm. At the time we are put to the test, he gives us the strength to endure, and so provides a way out (1 Cor. 10: 13).

When Paul tells us to pray in order to resist the Devil, he adds, 'Pray on every occasion, as the Spirit leads' (Eph. 6: 18). Earlier, we suggested that Paul's command to constant prayer as the Spirit leads referred to prayer in tongues. This is how the Spirit prays, 'in groans that words cannot express' (Rom. 8: 26). In the daily battle against Satan, prayer in God's language can be one of our most reliable weapons. For when the Spirit prays in us in this direct way, then Satan is disarmed.

Shirley was serving Christ in a foreign country where the prevailing religion was pagan. Soon, she and her colleagues became dramatically aware of the direct attacks of the Devil in a way they had never known before. They were troubled in their home by objects flying around for no natural reason. They were awakened at night by their names being called when no one was there. Only when they cleansed the house in the name of Jesus and painted the Cross over the symbols of pagan religion left by the previous owner did the attacks cease.

Few Christians will be attacked like that, but whatever the test the Enemy sends our way, prayer in tongues will always help us to overcome. Prayer is the all-round weapon we use to make all the others effective.

*When we fail*

Despite all the weapons God provides, from time to time we

shall fail in the spiritual conflict. Every Bible character except Jesus did, and every Christian great and small since Bible times has done too. Noah lay drunk and exposed in his tent after surviving the Flood (Gen. 9: 20-1). Abraham took his wife's slave to gain a son, instead of trusting God to keep his promise through Sarah herself (Gen. 16: 1-4). David seduced Bathsheba and murdered her husband after uniting the country under his rule and after his mighty victories over the Philistines (2 Sam. 11: 2-17). Peter compromised his faith after the Day of Pentecost and after working many miracles in Christ's name (Gal. 2: 11-14). Paul and Barnabas quarrelled and separated after all the triumphs of their first missionary journey together (Acts 15: 38-41).

Sinless perfection, this side of heaven, is not promised in the Bible. Victory is promised, and forgiveness is promised. John wrote his first letter so that his readers would not sin. 'But if anyone does sin, we have someone who pleads with the Father on our behalf – Jesus Christ the righteous one.' He is the means by which our sins are forgiven, and his power to forgive is endless (1 John 2: 1, 2).

So when you fall, fall on your knees. Be honest before God, in success and in failure. Come back to the cross. For 'the blood of Jesus purifies us from every sin' (1 John 1: 7). At the cross allow Jesus to wash you clean in his blood once more. Then accept God's forgiveness. So many Christians cannot forgive themselves when they sin, and so they reject God's forgiveness as well. But Christ is the means by which our sins are forgiven, so if we refuse to forgive ourselves, then we are rejecting him as well.

Sometimes private confession of our sins to God is not enough. 'Confess your sins to one another,' says James (Jas. 5: 16). Confession to others helps us to be honest. Sharing our failures with fellow Christians helps us to understand that our sins are not peculiar to ourselves; others are tempted as we are. They may have found ways of overcoming the temptations which they can share with us, to our mutual benefit.

When Jesus met his disciples on the first Easter Sunday

night, he breathed on them and said, 'Receive the Holy Spirit. If you forgive people's sins, they are forgiven; if you do not forgive them, they are not forgiven' (John 20: 22-3).

From this promise Christians have always understood that the church's ministry includes the authority to assure repentant and anxious sinners that they are truly forgiven in Jesus's name. So go to your minister, sometimes, when you have sinned and the feeling of forgiveness eludes you. He is there to help. And through the Holy Spirit he can give you back the joy of knowing you are God's child and will always have a place in his family.

When you fall, trust in Christ's work in heaven on your behalf. Christ's work of forgiveness did not end on the cross, vital as that was. Now he lives in heaven where he pleads with the Father for us. With such provision what have we to fear? Of course, we must not become lazy and slack, imagining we can sin as we please and then find God's forgiveness, but neither must we become depressed at our failure and imagine we are no longer true members of God's family. He is our Father, and he loves us for ever. Christ lives for ever to plead with God for us. When we fail we should accept his forgiveness and start again.

As Jesus approached the cross, his disciples were totally unaware of what was happening or of its meaning for the future of the world. All they could think of was their place in God's coming kingdom, which they still imagined would be some kind of earthly empire. That they were about to deny Christ and flee in terror from the soldiers who arrested him was, to them, totally unthinkable. But Jesus knew what was happening. He knew the depths of their failure and disloyalty to come. And he saw what they would ultimately become in the future, after the resurrection and his ascension to heaven.

'Simon, Simon! Listen!' Jesus said. 'Satan has received permission to test all of you, to separate the good from the bad, as a farmer separates the wheat from the chaff. But I have prayed for you, Simon, that your faith will not fail. And when you turn back to me, you must strengthen your brothers' (Luke 22: 31,32).

When Peter denied Jesus he 'went out and wept bitterly' (Luke 22: 62). No one could have failed more than he did. Yet Peter was gloriously restored. Six weeks later he preached the first Christian sermon and 3,000 people were baptised. Soon he was defending Jesus before the Jewish Council. Soon he was imprisoned and flogged for Christ's sake. Two of his letters have an honoured place in the New Testament. And, according to tradition, at the end of his life he was crucified upside down, because he said he was not worthy to be crucified the right way up as Jesus had been.

If Christ could restore Peter like that when he failed, then he can restore us as well. For Satan has demanded to have us, too, that he might sift us like wheat, but Christ prays for us, that our faith might not fail. And when we turn back to him, then he waits with renewed work for us to do for him.


*The healing power of Christ*

In their battle against Satan, many Christians find they are tempted by one or two particularly stubborn sins. In these areas of their lives promised victory eludes them. They cry with Paul, 'I don't do the good I want to do; instead I do the the evil that I do not want to do ... What an unhappy man I am! Who will rescue me from this body that is taking me to death?' (Rom. 7: 19, 24).

Temper is often one of these sins. No matter how hard we try, how much we pray, how often we confess and ask for forgiveness, from time to time we still lose our cool in situations which bring dishonour to Christ and leave us feeling guilty and ashamed. Sometimes particular situations at home or at work make us explosively angry. Sometimes particular individuals have the same effect. Sometimes we feel angry with ourselves deep down inside. We do not really

91

understand why, yet our anger boils over and is directed at others.

Some of us suffer from periods of depression for no apparent reason. Our joy in Christ leaves us. We feel worse than we did before we were born into God's family. We doubt if we belong to God at all. Some of us have problems with compulsive patterns of behaviour which lead us into sin. Others of us suffer from irrational fears which we are powerless to control. Again, because we often imagine that Christians are not supposed to feel or act like this we end up guilty and ashamed.

All these problems are among the fruits of sin. We have them because we are sinners by nature even after we have been born into God's family. But they are not all the result of deliberate wrongdoing. This is what makes them so distressing. We do not want to lose our tempers. We do not want to feel depressed or afraid of the dark. We do not want to keep behaving in potentially destructive ways, yet somehow we cannot help ourselves. The usual methods of confession and trust in Christ, activity in Christian service, Bible reading and prayer somehow do not seem to work. Is there anything that can be done?

First, we need to be totally honest about the real nature of our problem. Covering up for ourselves, blaming others, refusing to admit that something is really wrong will only make our problem worse. Thrusting it down will only suppress it for a while before it breaks out again with greater force and distress than before. Then we need to recognise that we are powerless to help ourselves. As long as we think we can cope, as long as we imagine we can handle ourselves we shall only compound our problem. 'I find that this law is at work,' says Paul: 'when I want to do what is good, what is evil is the only choice I have ... [I am] a prisoner to the law of sin which is at work in my body' (Rom. 7: 21, 23).

Secondly, we need to understand that when the Bible writers talk of sin they do not think simply in terms of wrongdoing. They think of sickness as well. Sin is not just the things I do that are wrong; it is the basic sickness of my human nature without God which leads me into wrongdoing in the first place. So often our 'sins' are not the root of our problem, they are its symptoms. Our explosive temper, our irrational fears, our periods of uncontrollable depression, our compulsive patterns of destructive behaviour are all expressions of a deep, inner sickness, and unless the sickness is healed we shall continue to be imprisoned by the law of sin which is at work in our bodies. Satan, the author of sin and the father of lies, will keep us bound.

This deep, inner sickness often finds its root in our childhood and infancy. Early experiences often leave emotional wounds and scars which continue to affect our personalities for the rest of our lives. Sometimes the root of the trouble is fairly easy to find. If we were abandoned by one or both of our parents because their marriage failed we may still feel bitter and rejected. A period in hospital at just the wrong time when we were very small, with a painful illness and even more painful treatment, can have left us with inexplicable fears.

Sometimes, the root of our trouble lies buried more deeply. Some psychiatrists have suggested that the very process of our birth can have left marks on our characters. Others have gone farther and traced feelings of rejection and utter worthlessness to the attitudes of our mothers towards us in the early months of our foetal lives. Not so many years ago, infants who were so emotionally bruised that they had lost the will to live simply sickened and died. Modern medicine prevents that from happening today, so proportionately more people bring deeply buried emotional problems to their adult lives with all their destructive consequences.

Jesus has dealt with the sickness which causes us to sin.

> Surely he has borne our sicknesses
>     and carried our pains; ...
> upon him was the chastisement that made us whole,
>     and with his stripes we are healed (Isa. 53: 4, 5 marg, RSV).

Jesus died on the cross, not only for our forgiveness, but for our healing.

So when we are beset with sins we cannot control, we can be confident that Christ can heal. If prayer and confession alone do not help, then we should share our problem with a minister or a professional counsellor, who, under the guidance of the Holy Spirit, can begin to lead us to its heart. 'Confess your sins to one another and pray for one another,' says James, 'so that you will be healed' (Jas. 5: 16).

So find someone who, under the Holy Spirit can go to the heart of your problem. You may need to forgive someone who has wronged you years before, a parent perhaps, or some other close relative. But with the inner healing that only Christ can give will come release from the emotional tension which has displayed itself in selfish and un-Christian ways.

This process of inner healing is rarely instantaneous and complete. When God by his Spirit uncovers one emotional wound and heals it, he often opens the way to another. But as we open ourselves to the breadth of his love, which is endless, and the searching power of his Spirit, so the ravages of sin and the power of Satan in our lives will be broken. 'Sin must not be your master; for you do not live under law but under God's grace' (Rom. 6: 14).

# CHAPTER 8– THE GROWING FAMILY

The young man sat nervously in the corner of the crowded railway compartment. In his pocket were some religious tracts. He believed it was the Christian's duty to 'witness' to everyone he met, and he meant to do it even if it killed him. The way he felt at present, that was what it was going to do, for he was very shy. But he had a plan. He was due to leave the train at Middlesbrough, whereas most of the travellers went through to Darlington. So he silently prayed throughout the journey. It was easy to be silent because he did not know any of them to speak to anyway. At last the signal-box marked Middlesbrough East flashed past the window. One minute to go. Now for it! Gulping with nervousness, he produced a fixed smile and a fistful of tracts.

'I'd like you to read one of these. They tell you how to get right with God,' he announced to a startled company. Quickly handing them around as the station platform slid into view, he said a bright 'Good morning' and scrambled out, gasping with relief. He had witnessed!

In actual fact he had probably done nothing of the sort. He had no natural contacts with his unwilling audience, he had not earned any right to speak to them, he had no knowledge of their interests, questions or personal condition. It was the most impersonal means of cummunication – 'give them something to read, and run.'

Not surprisingly, nothing came of the earnest endeavours which he practised in several successive compartments. But something else happened which surprised him very much. He left the train at Middlesbrough because he worked there in a factory. One day a fellow worker said to him, 'I notice you are different. You don't cuss. You don't tell dirty stories. You don't lose your temper. My six-year-old lass is very ill and has to see a specialist. Will you say a prayer for her when you go to church?'

Then a young man who brought him a sheaf of papers to sign each morning began to ask him questions. 'How do you keep up Christian living in a place like this? Sometimes I go to church, and the vicar's sermon stirs me up. I say, "Tony, you're going to be different." But it never lasts longer than Tuesday back in the factory. What is it you've got that I haven't?' The question led to a quick talk there and then, a longer conversation that evening. Next morning, to his friend's astonishment, he announced that he had asked Christ to be his Saviour. It worked. The passing years proved it.

Every Christian lives in a world of natural contacts. We have family relatives, school friends, workmates, fellow commuters, fellow students, neighbours. Other mums meet their children at the school gates, people bump into us playing squash, watching football, collecting train numbers or jogging. We meet people at parent-teacher associations, ratepayers' protest meetings, trade union meetings.

God has made these people our mission-field. Few of us will be called to dramatic pioneer missionary work. Not many of us are ordained to the ministry. But each of us is to be a witness. That was the last thing Jesus said before he returned to heaven (Acts 1: 7-8).

The plan      'You will be witnesses for me.'
The scope     'In Jerusalem, in all Judaea and Samaria, and to the ends of the earth.' (That is, in ever-widening circles, beginning nearest home.)
The secret    'When the Holy Spirit comes upon you, you will be filled with power.'

A witness is quite simply someone who shares the knowledge and experience which he has. In Britain's system of justice, the key to the whole thing is witnesses and testimony. So it is in God's plan for extending his family, building his kingdom and winning a verdict of 'yes' from a previously unbelieving world. In this plan, the Holy Spirit witnesses to the Christian. 'This Gospel is true,' he says to the believing heart. Because the Christian is a child of God, he has the God-given ability to receive and respond to that witness. 'Whoever believes in the Son of God has this testimony in his own heart' (1 John 5: 10). But the unbeliever cannot see or hear that testimony. He is spiritually dead, unresponsive and unheeding. So the witnessing Spirit speaks to him through the witnessing Christian. An unbeliever cannot see God or hear truth. But he can see how the Christian behaves and hear how he speaks. He can watch the reactions and hear the attitudes. He can see a quality of life and hear authentic reality. That is why our shy friend's workmate said 'pray for my child', 'how do you do it?' and eventually, 'show me Jesus'. Here is God's plan then. Jesus explained it. 'I will send him [the Helper] to you... he will prove to *the people of the world* that they are wrong' (John 16: 7-8).

Notice, this is not a job for some specialists. There are indeed specialists, including the evangelist: God's gift to the church with special abilities in communication, persuasiveness and spiritual power. But witnessing is for everyone. It is part of being a Christian. There is really no choice. Simply by living as Christians, we are being witnesses, either good ones or bad ones. Our living is quietly persuading people either that Jesus is alive or that religion is a bore and a fraud.

## How do I witness?

Probably the more consciously you try, the less effective you will be. Licking your lips nervously and trying to drag someone's conversation round to 'spiritual things' will look artificial and will likely cause embarrassment or resentment. The classic advice of the apostle Peter is simply: be ready when the natural opportunity comes. 'Be ready at all times to answer anyone who asks you to explain the hope you have in you, but do it with gentleness and respect' (1 Pet. 3: 15-16).

Poor Peter took a while to learn that himself. When a servant-girl asked him 'don't you know Jesus?' he was not ready, fumbled and collapsed. When a temple guard came looking for Jesus (not with the kindest of intentions) Peter acted without gentleness, and cut his ear off. First an extreme of defensiveness and then an extreme of offensiveness!

But Peter learned, and so may we. Far more people are prepared to ask and think than we sometimes believe. We must be ready when they do so, not struggling to set up artificial situations, but sensitive and responsive when the natural opportunity comes.

## What might I be asked?

Peter assumes that people will do the asking. They often will, if we give them the chance. Do them the courtesy of listening to them and taking them seriously. You will soon find that their questions repeatedly fall into familiar categories.

*There are questions raised by the media.* An enormous amount of spare time is spent watching television, listening to radio, and reading newspapers. 'Why does Mary Whitehouse keep interfering with people's pleasures?' 'Why doesn't the church speak out on issues?' Notice the splendid contradiction between those two questions, but both will often be asked, even by the same person.

'A bishop said on the radio this morning ...'

'My Sunday paper had the story of this minister who ran off with a Sunday School teacher ...'

'That Mother Teresa was on telly last night. Why do you think ...?'

'That earthquake in Iran – how can God allow it?'

Many of these questions will be superficial, confused and contradictory. That is in the nature of their source, unfortunately. But this is what shapes people's images. We must understand, respond with good humour and patience, learn to 'see ourselves as others see us'. Even failures and follies of 'the Church' (whatever they imagine it to be) can give us opportunity to be humble and realistic about Christian failures, and then to lead on to something positive.

'All right, we Christians often fail. Then tell me, is it better to have a high standard and sometimes fail to reach it, or a standard so low that no one would either miss it or even notice it?'

'Yes, OK, there are some hypocrites in the church. But what is a hypocrite? An imitation of the real thing. You only imitate something worth while. People forge five-pound notes; no one forges bits of brown paper. Doesn't it mean something that Christianity is worth forging?'

'I know we often let our side down. But the Gospel isn't for perfect people. It's for the bad guys. My only qualification for being accepted by God is that I'm not good enough. You don't see what I mean? Let me show you what Jesus said ...'

*There are questions raised by life's experiences.* A disaster takes many lives and is reported in the media. More personal loss of grief is experienced. The questions inevitably arise. Why? An almost invariable part of serious conversation will be this question. 'How can a God of love ...?' There is no easy answer, but if we are to get anywhere in sharing our faith we must learn to offer some part-answers. They will depend on the type of person asking the question, the attitude being shown, and the nature of the suffering involved.

We can try to answer logically. Being human at all involves free will. God did not make us puppets with strings pulled by him, or machines with buttons pressed by him. We go our own way, make our own choices, take our own risks, and God lets us. The consequences come. 'You still think he ought to intervene at some point? Prevent you from stepping in front of a bus? Keep you off the plane that crashes? Bounce the virus off somewhere else? Very well – are you ready to be consistent? If he is going to pull the strings, do you welcome him to pull them all? Can he stop you telling lies? Can he intervene with your sex-life? Can he compel you to observe Sunday?'

We can try to answer personally. We may have an experience of our own to relate. How we felt when we were in hospital. How we had God's peace in the bereavement. Or we know someone else's testimony and can relate it.

We can try to answer theologically. 'Yes, suffering is a great mystery. I don't know why God has allowed it. But I do know this. God has not kept aloof from it, a million miles away in space. In Jesus, he came here and suffered, suffered with us and for us. That's what the cross is about. I can never look at the cross and then say, God doesn't care.'

We can try to answer eschatologically (though it would be unwise to use the word!). As long as we think of the whole meaning of life as being compressed between the cradle and the grave, we shall never get it right. God has long-term plans. A better day is coming. Christ will return, and there'll be no nonsense next time about throwing him out. 'You don't like pie in the sky? Well I'm sorry – you asked me how a Christian sees suffering, and the Christian has got pie in the sky. You stick to blood in the mud if you prefer it.'

*There are questions raised by death.* The possibility of life after death never ceases to fascinate people. Catering for it is a growth industry today. Some of it is dangerous and destructive; interest in spiritualism, ghosts, the occult, is enormous. There are (more safely) growing evidences from medical circles of consciousness after clinical death. We need to know how to handle these issues. More important, we need to understand the Bible's answer. Try to introduce a realisation that Christianity is concerned with quality and not merely survival. Eternal life is not a pale ghostly existence after death, but something begun now which is so glorious and full and dynamic that death cannot destroy it. The Bible in fact says little about living in heaven when we

100

die, but much about sharing life with Christ, now and later. And the Christian certainty of life after death is based, not on psychic evidence or hopeful parallels with winter and spring, but on the historical fact that Jesus rose from the dead.

When answering any of these questions, we need to bear something vital in mind. We should always look for some response, but the nature of that response will vary. Unless you have the definite and proven gifts of the evangelist, you are not often likely to conclude a conversation with the words, 'Would you like to kneel now and ask Christ into your life?' A much more frequent suggestion will be –

'How about coming round to my flat for a coffee and chat next week?'

'May I lend you this book? It puts it well.'

'Would you care to come to our church with me on Sunday?'

'My minister (youth leader/house-group leader/CU secretary) is very easy to talk to. Let me know if you'd like his advice.'


*How else can I witness effectively?*

Witnessing is not just a matter of words, of easy conversation and clever argument. With these alone we shall win few people for Jesus Christ. Our witnessing in words must be supported in other ways as well.

*1 We must live consistent Christian lives.* 'I can't hear what you're saying: your actions are shouting too loudly!' is an all-too-common complaint made against over-zealous Christians. The Pharisees were full of religious observance, religious teaching and religious argument yet Jesus called them hypocrites because of the inconsistencies in their lives. In the same way, if our lives are inconsistent, our witnessing will only turn people away from Christ instead of drawing them to him.

The hardest place to witness is at home, particularly when other members of our families do not share our faith in Jesus. They know all our faults. Constant badgering about Christ will only alienate them, but consistent Christian living will challenge them. Paul was in his mid-teens. One summer he went to a Christian camp for his holiday and while he was there, he accepted Christ as his personal Saviour. When he returned home he joined a local church and started attending its services and youth fellowship. Six months later, his mother sought out his minister. 'I don't know what happened to our Paul when he went away on holiday last summer,' she said, 'but I can't get over the way he's been different ever since. I want what he's got.' Paul had never said a word; perhaps he should have done. But the consistency of his Christian life became his best testimony and that, in turn led his mother to Christ.

Writing to wives, married to unbelieving husbands, Peter says, 'submit ... so that ... your conduct will win them over to believe. It will not be necessary for you to say a word, because they will see how pure and reverent your conduct is' (1 Pet. 3: 1, 2). Christian wives who nag their husbands for their lack of faith, who are out every night of the week at some church activity or other and who adopt an unyielding attitude to the way they spend Sunday should not be surprised if their husbands become embittered against Christ and his church, and maybe seek solace in the arms of someone else. Christian teenagers who stay out late, who never help at home but expect to be waited on hand and foot by long-suffering parents, who are mean with the amount of their earned income they hand over for their keep, and who justify their selfish behaviour by appealing to their supposed commitment to Jesus Christ, bring more dishonour on his Name than honour. They cannot complain if their well-meaning and bemused parents fear they are suffering from religious mania! Christian parents who neglect their growing children through involvement in a host of worthy Christian activities, and expect their families to tag along to one boring meeting after another cannot wonder when their children turn their backs on Jesus as soon as they are finally old enough to do so. Witnessing is about living before it is about speaking.

The second hardest place to witness is at work. Here again, the strains and stresses of close contact with the same group of people week after week and month after month, coupled with the tiring activity of work itself expose our faults and weaknesses. Christians are particularly vulnerable. If they rightly refuse to contribute to the weekly sweepstake or the annual Christmas binge they run the risk of adopting a 'holier-than-thou' attitude. If they then slack at work, take Monday off because they are exhausted after Sunday, set themselves up as moral arbiters of their colleagues' behaviour, they bring disrepute on Christ's name.

Sally was a student nurse. The ward sister was of the old school, a rigid disciplinarian and a tartar for punctuality. When she ticked Sally off for being persistently late in the morning, Sally flared up: 'I'm a Christian! I take my orders from the Lord, not you!' She was wrong. She served the Lord by obeying the staff and caring for the patients. She proved a failure at nursing, so finished up neither recommending the Lord nor helping others.

Bert worked in the accounts office. Nationalisation and restructuring were causing frayed nerves and short tempers. When he was about to be moved to another department, Bert was approached by the chief clerk: 'I just want to say that you're a gentleman: the way you react when the girls get something wrong, the good-natured grin when you turn down the office lottery, the patience you show on the telephone with an awkward customer. I hear you're a local preacher. I'd like to hear you. Where are you due on Sunday?'

Writing to slaves, the first-century equivalent of modern employees, Paul told them to consider their masters worthy of all respect, 'so that no one will speak evil of the name of God and of our teaching' (1 Tim. 6: 1). They should work cheerfully, 'as though you served the Lord, and not merely men' (Eph. 6: 7). When we behave like this, our witnessing will be effective, for people will want to hear what we have to say.

*2 We must expect God to work.* Witnessing will often be bitterly disappointing. If we are not derided or scorned we shall often simply be ignored. Even if some show temporary interest, it may quickly pass. Weeks may pass when no natural opportunities to speak for Christ will occur. Before we know where we are we may feel we have joined the ranks of the silent majority of silent Christians who, in true British fashion, keep their religion to themselves.

In all our discouragement we must not give up. Our witnessing, in itself, will never bring anyone to Christ but, under the Holy Spirit, it will often prove to be a step along the way. Recalling how the Corinthians became strong in Christ, Paul says, 'I sowed the seed, Apollos watered the plant, but it was God who made the plant grow' (1 Cor. 3: 6). If we expect God to work, he will. If we believe he will use our words and actions to bring people into his family, he will.

Often when we are ignored or contradicted, people go away and think about what we have said. They may come back with a different attitude. They may meet someone else who will follow up what we have said with just the right reply. They do not know how apt their comment is, but God is at work. And so, little by little, people come to the moment of birth into new life in Jesus.

*3 We must pray in the Holy Spirit.* If we want to be effective witnesses for Christ, we must cultivate the habit of praying for our natural contacts. Many of us find this surprisingly difficult. We are still basically so selfish that we pray mainly for ourselves and our own concerns and forget the needs of others. Yet how can we expect natural opportunities for witness to arise unless we ask for them? So we need to keep praying for people we meet regularly, and people with obvious needs, that a chance to share Christ with them will present itself.

*4 We must gain the support of our local church.* We cannot grow as Christians on our own. Neither can we witness effectively by ourselves. In our prayers for opportunities to witness we must enlist the support of others. Our aim is not merely to witness to Jesus Christ, but to bring new-born spiritual babies into his family. Unless we belong to a branch of that family where the new-born can easily grow we shall become frustrated with disappointment as one after another start to grow in Christ and then lose their faith.

Indeed, God has put us in local communities of Christians because it is through them that he prefers to work. In a sense, every special town-wide mission, every specialist group, every missionary society is a confession that local churches are not doing their job properly.

The wandering ministry of the early apostles wrought wonders. But almost more wonderful was the effective witnessing of anonymous and unsung Christian groups who declared simply by the way they lived that Jesus was Lord. In Syria, ordinary Christians gossiped the Gospel, broke the race barrier between Jews and Gentiles, and reminded people so much of Christ that the nickname 'Christian' was invented (Acts 11: 19-26). In Greece, the life-style displayed in newly-planted churches caused more of a sensation than the preaching of the apostles (1 Thess. 1: 5-10). The mighty and corrupt city of Rome itself was captured for Christ long before Paul arrived, apparently by a natural witness borne through unknown Christians developing their church life.

A local church can offer a corporate expression, visible to people's eyes, of the meaning and proof of the Christian Gospel. When Christians worship God together with unaffected enthusiasm and joy, the unbeliever asks questions about God. When different classes, cultures and colours are merged in one community, the good news of reconciliation with God is declared in the fact that we are reconciled with each other. When caring, sharing and fellowship are displayed, a world groaning in its loneliness and lost identity sits up and takes notice. When personality quirks are being ironed out, emotional disorders healed and welcoming arms extended, a society full of the casualties of permissive behaviour takes notice. When clear preaching of the Gospel is confirmed by godly living, people will listen. When meetings for prayer are marked by vision, compassion and expectancy (and prayers are answered!) those around are forcefully reminded that God is alive. For all these reasons, your effectiveness in witnessing will therefore depend, to some extent, on the full and loyal part you play in the life of your local church.

A silent Christian is a disobedient Christian. Christians who are ashamed of Jesus will find he will be ashamed of them on the day when he comes again in the glory of his father (Mark 8: 38). If you have never witnessed for Christ, ask him for the strength and courage to begin. If your witness has been spasmodic and largely ineffective, pray for natural opportunities to share him with others. 'Be ready at all times to answer anyone who asks you to explain the hope you have in you, but do it with gentleness and respect' (1 Pet. 3: 15-16).

# CHAPTER 9 – THE FAMILY FIRM

There was a buzz of interest in the foundry. Young Master Harry, second son of the Old Man who ran the firm from his upstairs office, was back from university. Production manager, he was to be called. 'Fancy name for a gaffer who gets more out of us,' grumbled one workman, but he was grinning. Mister Edward, the elder son, was already running the Accounts Department. His wife did a good job overseeing the works canteen. For it was a family firm. The Old Man's late father had started it long ago, and each member of the family had found his or her place in it ever since. They were proud of their name, proud of their products, jealous of their reputation and good to their employees. They expected hard work, and the set-up was small enough for them to spell out its economics to their men. On the whole, they succeeded. One reason was that the Old Man and his sons knew how to work hard themselves. They were first in, in the morning, and last out at night. They took work home at the weekends. For they were not just employees. They were The Family. They had their own business: the Family Firm.

That kind of thing is in decline today. Multinational business empires, consortium monopolies, supermarket chains selling brand names, nationalised industries; size and anonymity are the order of the day. Whatever the political rights and wrongs, most older people recall with regret the passing of that personal interest, pride in work and constructive commitment that went with the family business at its best.

When we are born into the family of God, we are also

recruited into the Family Firm. For God our Father has great plans for his world. Through his Son, he has decided to bring the whole universe back to himself. Through Christ's death on the cross he has forgiven a world in rebellion against him, and in his eternal plan he has already brought it back to himself (Col. 1: 20). And in order to accomplish his plan, God has set up a firm. He is its Master, Christ is its head and all Christians are given individual positions within it. That firm is the Christian church. It is the only means God has given himself to restore a lost and fallen world. What an amazing thing! God has determined to realise his eternal purpose for his universe through you and all the other members of his family world wide.

Before he ascended into heaven, Jesus set out the prospectus for the family firm. He gave it the stamp of his personal authority, for he has been given all authority in heaven and on earth. 'Go, then,' he said, 'to all peoples everywhere and make them my disciples: baptise them in the name of the Father, the Son, and the Holy Spirit, and teach them to obey everything I have commanded you' (Matt. 28: 19-20).

This is the church's task; proclaiming Christ throughout the world, winning people to follow him, baptising them into the family of God and teaching them to obey all Christ's commands. The church acts with the authority of Christ himself, and as it acts it enjoys his presence, for he said, 'And I will be with you always, to the end of the age' (Matt. 28: 20).

Christians cannot accomplish the church's task by personal witnessing alone, important as that is. Over and above the personal witness which every Christian should bear to Christ, the church must be organised to accomplish the Great Commission. Some must evangelise, some must plant churches, some must teach. Others must heal the sick, for healing is part of the gospel of Christ. Others must work for the removal of injustice in society for Christ came to set free the oppressed. Others must strive for the rehabilitation of offenders, for Christ was sent to proclaim liberty to the captives. The removal of prejudice, apathy, ignorance and intolerance is also in the prospectus, for Christ came to give recovery of sight to the blind. The time has come when the Lord will save his people, and the church is the instrument of that salvation (Luke 4: 18-19).

## Gifts for the body of Christ

In order that the church might succeed in its task God, by his Spirit, has poured out gifts on its members. Some are gifts of leadership and position enabling Christians to plant new churches, to speak God's message, to evangelise, to care for and teach others (Eph. 4: 11). Others are gifts of service, the ability to encourage others, to share generously, and to show kindness to others (Rom. 12: 7-8). Others still are gifts of supernatural insight and power: the ability to give messages full of wisdom and knowledge, the ability to exercise faith in the mighty power of God to handle specific situations, the power to heal and to work miracles, the ability to tell the difference between gifts that come from the Spirit and those that do not, the ability to speak in tongues and the ability to explain what is said.

All these gifts are given by God's Spirit, as he wishes, to Christians to enable them to strengthen Christ's church in order that it might fulfil its world-wide task. Some Christians have many gifts. All Christians have one or more gifts. Christians should not envy the gifts of others nor should they despise those with fewer gifts than themselves or less spectacular gifts than their own. For the Christian church is like a body with Christ as its head and all its members as different limbs and organs within it. Just as a human body need all its different parts to work smoothly together if it is to function efficiently, so the church needs all its members to exercise their gifts if it is to grow and proclaim Christ to the world.

When we are born into God's family, therefore, we should not see our responsibility towards others simply in terms of personal witnessing, important as that is. We should want to

109

become actively involved in the work of Christ's church, in the task of bringing the Good News of Jesus to everyone in the world. Of ourselves we cannot do this. Anything we attempt for Christ, in our own strength, will come to nothing. We need the gifts of the Holy Spirit. 'Earnestly desire the spiritual gifts,' says Paul (1 Cor. 14: 1 RSV). So we should begin to pray that God will give us, by his Spirit, those abilities that he knows are best for us. In this way we shall find a natural place in the ongoing work of the church wherever we are.

Sometimes, God's gifts will be extensions of our natural talents. It is useful if the church treasurer has some financial expertise already or the bookstall secretary knows something about selling techniques. But often, because God is God, he gives new gifts, totally unexpected, in order to display the sovereign power of his Spirit. So the shy and timid introvert becomes an exuberant and successful evangelist. The one-time slow learner discovers an unknown facility with languages enabling him to work effectively in the Third World.

Sometimes, God's gifts come in response to the deep longings of our hearts that something should be done about a desperate situation which everyone else ignores. When Thomas John Barnardo, as a young medical student in Victorian London, first learned of the thousands of homeless boys and girls sleeping rough on the streets of the capital every night, he little thought that one day he would head a national network of orphanages caring for hundreds of thousands of children. But he found, as he prayed that God would do something to meet the children's needs, that God answered his prayers through him, and through his obedience to God's call.

The same sort of thing happened, at a far less spectacular level, when Stephen said to his minister father one day, 'Dad, I'm really burdened about evangelism. I think God is calling me to it, but I don't seem to be a preacher, and there's no way I could give up my job ...'

'I know only one way to measure evangelism, son,' replied

his father. 'Are folk being converted? It's as simple as that. If you think you are called to evangelism, pray for conversions, and pray for contacts that will lead to conversions.'

Stephen prayed for six months. Then a secular youth club was hard pressed for leaders and asked him to help. As he superintended games, served squash, organised outings, the members began to ask him about his faith. Why did he not swear? Why was he never in the pub? Why was he such fun to be with? He invited four of them home for coffee and questions. They began to study the Bible at a very simple level. A couple went to his church and eventually found faith. A weekly house-meeting began for Bible reading and prayer. Now twenty-five members meet regularly; most of them are new believers.

Some of the Spirit's gifts bear no relation to our natural abilities whatsoever. Gifts of wisdom, prophecy and knowledge, the ability to bring a message in tongues and the ability to interpret that message are sometimes given to the most unlikely of people. But the Spirit wants everyone to play their part in the strengthening and upbuilding of Christ's church. The power to heal, discernment of the presence of evil spirits, insights of faith into the activity of God in particular and crucial situations; these are sometimes given regularly, but often only very occasionally to meet special needs at certain times.

Some of God's gifts are spectacular. Others are unseen and unheard. We need to be willing to receive both if we are to fulfil our God-appointed role in the ministry of his church. In all probability, the greatest saints are not the Billy Grahams and Mother Teresas of this world with their international ministries and acclaim, but the unsung heroes and heroines who exercise their humble gifts in secret and whom God will one day reward openly.

Lily's church was involved in a rebuilding programme costing thousands of pounds. From the pulpit, one Sunday morning, the minister urged everyone in the congregation to give fifty pounds towards the rebuilding fund. 'If you cannot give fifty,' he said, 'give what you can and ask God for the

rest.' Lily went home, bitter and angry. How dare the
minister ask her, a widow in reduced circumstances, to give
fifty pounds! Then she remembered what he had said, 'If you
cannot give fifty, give what you can and ask God for the rest.'
Opening her purse and counting her money, Lily set aside
five pounds, closed her eyes, and asked God to make it up to
fifty. The following morning, to her total surprise, the
postman dropped an envelope from an unknown source
through her letter box: it contained exactly forty-five
pounds! For Lily, that became the start of the exercise of a
new gift. In the weeks and months that followed, she gave
away hundreds and thousands of pounds to various
Christian causes and individuals. Little of the money was her
own, for she had none. But when she saw a need she asked
God to meet it, and he met it in the same way as he had
provided the original forty-five pounds. Very few people
ever knew about her gift of faith and generosity. She gave in
secret and God rewarded her,

## Serving God in the local church

Most of us, when we are born into God's family, will begin to
find the use of our spiritual gifts in our local church. Here,
there is a constant need for new workers. Sunday School
teachers, playgroup leaders and helpers, new house-group
leaders, those willing to share their faith in the homes of
others are always in short supply. Good churches are always
looking for fresh blood to serve on their councils and
diaconates. Singers, musicians, magazine distributors, those
willing to maintain and repair the church fabric are all
needed if the church is to function efficiently. Youth club
leaders are usually more than grateful for the help of new
assistants with vision and fresh ideas. Prayer groups keep the
church and its constituent parts in touch with God;
willingness to spend time in prayer with others is vital. Most
churches nowadays encourage some members of their
congregations to share in leading the worship and preaching.

Special training may be necessary here; are we willing for the sacrifice in time and effort which may be involved?

Outside the boundaries of the local church itself are other opportunities for Christian service. One may feel passionately about the divisions in the church and so become active in the local Council of Churches. Another may become appalled at the threat to peace and so join a local peace group working for disarmament. Yet another may relieve the needs of the sick and elderly through the Women's Royal Voluntary Service. Another may bring a Christian mind to bear on political issues through membership of a political party and a local council. Another may become a prison visitor, another may become a marriage guidance counsellor. Some of these things are not exclusively Christian, but Christians have a proper place in them, for through their work they can display the presence and compassion of Christ. Quite rightly, many Christians are responding to appeals from local authorities to become foster parents. Through many heartaches, and only with the love of Jesus, they begin to rebuild young, bruised and broken lives, and sometimes, after much tact and patience, they see their foster children come to know Jesus too.

Sometimes, Christians become so wrapped up in the work of their local church that they lose all contact with the non-Christian world outside. That should never happen for then they are disobeying the Great Commission to take the Gospel to every creature. But when we become Christians our lives are changed, not only in their characteristics, but in the way we spend our time and money. Through Christian service in our local church and community we grow in Christ, for we have to rely on him to equip us for the work to which he has called us, and when we do, we find he does not disappoint us.

*Serving God 'full time'*

On joining God's family most people remain in the situation

113

they were in before their new birth. Those who are at school or college continue with their studies. Those at work continue in their employment. Their attitude to work should change, as we outlined in the previous chapter, and they should witness to Christ among their colleagues. Many Christians will continue in so-called secular work for the rest of their lives, making their secular calling divine by their honesty, sincerity, integrity and hard work. But for others, birth into God's family will bring change in the way they earn their living, sometimes quickly, sometimes after many years.

Some work, by its very nature, is dubious for the Christian to follow. The tobacco industry and the liquor trade probably come into this category, for their overall effects on others are generally harmful rather than beneficial. Gambling poses similar problems through its encouragement of greed and its deeply destructive effects on the individuals who become addicted to it and conflict with the Christian's obedience to Christ.

Sometimes, different Christians will come to different conclusions. Some Christians in sport, for instance, see nothing inconsistent with their Christian profession and playing or servicing the game on Sundays. Others find the Sunday involvement a real crisis of conscience and may retire from the game as a result. Eric Liddell's story, recently popularised in the film, *Chariots of Fire*, has come as a welcome reminder of the standards British Christians once brought to this vexed issue. In the 'twenties and 'thirties Eric Liddell was not alone in the stand he took; Jack Hobbs similarly refused to play Sunday cricket in Australia because he did not wish to embarrass and hinder the work of the churches there. Sport is not the only area of work, of course, with an increasing Sunday involvement. As society becomes increasingly secularised more and more people are being expected and required to work on Sundays. In the future, more and more Christians are likely to be faced with the agonising choice between earning their living in a particular employment and keeping the Sabbath day holy.

Conflict between a Christian's work and his obedience to Christ may come in other ways. Peter was manager of a store with large-scale tax evasion and dishonest sources of supply built into its structure. After he became a Christian he could no longer encourage, or even turn a blind eye to, what was going on. He boldly asked the owner to change his style. When he refused Peter had to go – into unemployment for several months.

Not only, however, do Christians face choice between their work and their obedience to Christ on moral grounds. Because the Christian church is a family firm, committed to making Christ's love known throughout the world, Christians have always been prominent in the 'caring' professions. Most of them – free medical care, universal education, the probation service, care of children, the poor and the elderly – were started by Christians in the first place. As they grow in God's family, many Christians find they are being pulled away from perfectly honourable and respectable forms of work to serving their fellow men in one of these fields. When the time for decision comes, to retrain, to take a cut in salary, to move to a smaller house in a less desirable neighbourhood, it can be every bit as agonising as the choice between right and wrong faced by others.

Then specifically Christian charities and other agencies are always on the lookout for employees. Bible translation and distribution, evangelism among children, young people and adults, producing Christian literature, music and visual aids all demand full-time Christian employment and some Christians will be called into these fields. Here the financial cost may be greater still, for most Christian agencies depend on voluntary giving by other Christians for their income, and therefore they have to spend as carefully as possible. Some agencies give no financial guarantees to their workers at all, but ask them to depend on God in day-to-day faith to meet their material needs. When a Christian begins to feel God's call into one of these areas his faith and commitment can be tested to the limit.

No Christian should ever enter this kind of 'full-time

service' without the clearest certainty of God's call. This call should be confirmed by the active support and encouragement of others. No Christian should work as a Christian because he has nothing else to do, or because he has failed in secular employment. The Christian who cannot hold down an ordinary job is no more likely to hold down a 'Christian' job, for the stresses and strains are greater, not less. The Christian who has never survived in the harsh, real world of secular employment will rarely be effective in full-time Christian work.

Over and above the many 'Christian' jobs which the church provides in order to take the Gospel to every creature, comes the call to the Christian ministry itself. Everything we have said so far applies here in ever greater degree. If the minister is married, his or her partner must share his call, for the work demands total commitment, round the clock, whenever the minister and his family are at home. Few ministers scale the glamorous heights of the international circuit, of regular preaching to hundreds of avid listeners, of seeing dramatic church growth which wins universal acclaim. All ministers spend hours with desperately demanding and needy people often with seemingly incurable ills. All ministers hear heartrending confessions which have to be kept in strictest confidence. All ministers know loneliness, tiredness, disappointment, rejection and periods of dryness. Without the call of God and the constant strengthening and sustaining of his Spirit, the minister will fail and will bring ruin on the church he longs to serve. But God calls, and when he calls, we must obey.

## Serving God overseas

Christ's commission to his disciples was to go 'into all the world', to preach the gospel, 'to all mankind', to 'make disciples of all nations'. 'You will be witnesses for me in Jerusalem, in all Judaea and Samaria, and to the ends of the earth' (Acts 1: 8). The family firm is a world-wide firm with a world-wide task.

Two hundred years ago a sickly teenage cobbler in Northamptonshire was seized with the call of the Great Commission. The English church of his day was decadent, riddled with unitarian heresy and humanist reason, and dying on its feet. The Baptist group to which William Carey the cobbler belonged was small, poor and despised. When the cobbler became a minister he was so poor that his congregation had to have a whip round to buy him a pulpit suit! When he shared his world-wide vision with his fellow ministers he was scorned and derided. 'Sit down, young man!' he was told at one ministers' meeting. 'When God wants to save the heathen he'll do so without your help!'

Yet in due time, William Carey formed a missionary society, sailed with his wife as its first missionary to Calcutta, planted the Christian church in Bengal, translated the Bible or parts of it into a score of oriental languages and founded a Christian university which continues to the present day. From William Carey's pioneering efforts the church's missionary movement can be dated.

Throughout the nineteenth century hundreds and thousands of British Christians sailed to the ends of the earth and penetrated the hearts of its remotest islands and continents with the Gospel of Christ. In the twentieth century they have been joined by hundreds and thousands more, mainly from North America. Now increasingly, the church's world-wide task is being shared by the church world wide.

Yet the needs of the church overseas continue unabated. No longer the colonial missionary, lording it over the poor and untrained natives, but genuine partners in Christ, working beside and under the direction of local leadership, are needed throughout the Third World. Bible translation, leadership training, medical and educational work, famine relief, agricultural work, training in radio and television; for these and many other tasks missionary societies are still seeking recruits. The sacrifice involved is high, financial

117

rewards meagre, but the joy of obeying God's will surpasses them all.

Eight hundred years before Jesus was born a young Jewish priest had a vision of God in the Temple in Jerusalem. Overwhelmed with the sight of God's majesty, power and holiness he cried, 'There is no hope for me!' Then an angel touched his lips with a glowing coal from the altar, pronounced him free from guilt and forgiven of his sin. Then Isaiah heard the Lord say, 'Whom shall I send? Who will be our messenger?' He answered, 'I will go! Send me!' (Isa. 6: 1-8)

Perhaps God is calling you, as you read this book. He wants you to leave your comfortable job with its ample salary, bright prospects and guaranteed index-linked pension. He wants you to serve him, directly, in your employment. He wants you in community work, or caring for the aged, or serving him overseas. He is calling you into the ministry of his church, into a full-time job with the family firm. 'Whom shall I send?' he asks. 'Who will be our messenger?' Will you answer, 'I will go! Send me!'?

# CHAPTER 10 – HEIRS TOGETHER

Esther was single and on the verge of middle life. Somehow, when she was young the chance to marry had passed her by. Now, she lived with her widowed mother in a modest, suburban home. One way and another, she made friends with Jack who lived next door. Very shy, he was single and middle-aged too, still living with ageing parents.

Esther took Jack to church where he found a simple faith in Christ. When he finally plucked up the courage to ask her to marry him she gladly said, 'Yes.' To the great delight of all their friends a new home was bought and the nuptial knot was tied. Littered with confetti, Esther and Jack set off for their honeymoon and the adventure of married life together. While they were away, Jack was taken ill and brought home by ambulance to the local hospital. There, three months later, he died, from a tumour on his brain.

Why? Why should Esther wait so long to meet the man of her dreams only to have him snatched away so cruelly?

Anthony and Christine met at university where they were students together. When they realised they were in love they planned to marry, and so they did when their courses finished. From the start, their marriage was built on faith in Christ and obedience to his commands. Within a couple of years Anthony and Christine were thrilled to discover they were expecting their first child. Yes, there was a slight complication in Christine's condition, but it should cause no problems.

In due time, to Anthony and Christine's great delight, Benjamin was born. Almost immediately, however, he was taken from them as the doctors and nurses began to fight for his life. Despite constant reassurance, their efforts failed; within twelve hours of birth, Benjamin's tiny life had come to an end.

Why? Why should that happen to Anthony and Christine, who were so devoted to each other, and who would have made such excellent parents?

Lots of people imagine that when they become Christians all their troubles will end, all their problems will be solved. In fact, the opposite is the case. At the end of their first missionary journey, Paul and Barnabas returned to the towns where they had planted infant churches. They strengthened the believers and encouraged them to remain true to the faith. '"We must pass through many troubles to enter the Kingdom of God" they taught' (Acts 14: 22).

Like everyone else, Christians live in a suffering world. Hunger and heartbreak, sickness and grief, conflict and unemployment, exploitation and injustice, are all part of the human lot. Nowehere does the Bible suggest that Christians will be any more immune from these troubles than others. Indeed, some Christians will seem to suffer far more than they should, or deserve.

Besides the natural suffering which Christians share with everyone else, they must also expect to suffer as Christians. Jesus said, 'If anyone wants to come with me he must forget self, carry his cross, and follow me' (Mark 8: 34). Someone carrying a cross in Jesus's day was facing the most painful form of execution ever devised by man. We must expect that, once we start to follow Jesus.

'Happy are you,' said Jesus, 'when people insult you and persecute you and tell all kinds of evil lies against you because you are my followers' (Matt. 5: 11). 'You will be arrested and handed over to be punished and be put to death. All mankind will hate you because of me' (Matt. 24: 9). 'The time will come when anyone who kills you will think that by doing this he is serving God' (John 16: 2).

Jesus's warnings are repeated in the rest of the New Testament. 'Everyone who wants to live a godly life in union with Christ Jesus', Paul wrote to Timothy, 'will be persecuted' (2 Tim. 3: 12). 'Do not be surprised at the painful test you are suffering, as though something unusual were happening to you,' wrote Peter. 'Rather be glad ...' (1 Pet. 4: 12-13).

## The trial of your faith

Christians suffer that their faith might be strengthened. 'The trials you suffer,' says the apostle Peter, are 'to prove that your faith is genuine. Even gold, which can be destroyed, is tested by fire; and so your faith, which is much more precious than gold, must also be tested, so that it may endure' (1 Pet. 1: 7).

If Christians never suffered their faith would never grow. Life would be so easy that they would just take Jesus and his blessings for granted. They would become like spoiled children, demanding this and that, and always getting what they wanted. A perennial problem in the Third World is the problem of 'rice Christians'. Rice Christians are people who have attached themselves to the church for the material benefits they can gain from overseas. Their faith is spurious, at best secondhand, for when the overseas aid is withdrawn, they, in turn, withdraw their allegiance to Christ. If we never had to contend with suffering and disappointment, our faith would quickly become like that.

When many people suffer they blame God for what has happened. Christians can sometimes fall into the same trap as well. 'Why should God do this to me?' they cry. 'What have I done to deserve this?' Suffering, of course, almost always is unfair and undeserved. That is why it is so agonising. And the strongest Christians are usually those who have suffered most. In their suffering they have found that Christ has been there. He has not left them nor deserted them.

Mary's husband left her with three young children to care for. Despite a court settlement he rarely sent the maintenance that was decided. The anxiety and strain were too much. Mary ended up in hospital and the children went into care. For months on end, Mary's breakdown was so total she physically attacked any man who went near her. Yet afterwards she said that in the depths of her despair she knew that Christ was with her. Today, she is fully restored, strong and happy in a new marriage, a constant strength and encouragement to all who are depressed, for she has been there, and Christ has been there and brought her through.

Often the strongest Christians are those who have suffered most. Eliazaro lived in Kenya during the 1950s when the Mau Mau were leading the fight for independence against British rule. They recruited members by subjecting them to pagan rites and blood sacrifices. When Christians refused to submit, out of loyalty to Jesus, they were often cruelly tortured and killed.

For three years Eliazaro returned home from work each night, wondering if he would find a note pinned to his door, a note serving notice of Mau Mau intention to recruit. He never found the note, but he so learned to walk with Jesus that the joy and light of Jesus's presence became integral to his whole way of life.

So, says Peter, be glad, even though it may now be necessary for you to be sad for a while because of the many kinds of trial you suffer. For when you suffer you prove that your faith is genuine and strong (1 Pet. 1: 6-9).


*The strengthening of your character*

Another reason why Christians suffer is to refine their characters. A certain amount of suffering is necessary in everyone's life in order to make them strong and resilient, upright and good. All children have to suffer, through discipline, to this end, and the same is true in the Christian life. 'Trouble produces endurance, endurance brings God's approval, and his approval creates hope' (Rom. 5: 3-4).

The author of the Letter to the Hebrews develops this theme in particular. Jesus himself, even though he was God's Son, learned through his sufferings to be obedient, he says

(Heb. 5: 8). In the same way, Christians themselves must expect to suffer because 'your suffering shows that God is treating you as his sons' (Heb. 12: 7). Human fathers punish their children because they love them and need to correct them; why should God treat his children any differently? God disciplines us 'so that we may share his holiness' (Heb. 12: 10). Naturally, at the time, suffering is unpleasant. 'Later, however, those who have been disciplined ... reap the peaceful reward of a righteous life' (Heb. 12: 11).

So suffering can have a negative or a positive effect. It can make us hard, embittered and cynical, or it can make us more and more like Jesus. If we resent trouble and hardship, if we blame God for it, or if we blame others, we shall become full of anger and self-pity. But if we learn that all our lives are governed and controlled by a God who loves us, then we can become forgiving and accepting and find our characters strengthened as a result.

Various readers will be suffering in various ways. Some will be unemployed, some will be bereaved. Some will be financially poor. Some will have been hurt by unkindness and injustice. Some will be weighed down by disappointment and anxiety. Whatever we are going through, God knows. Whatever has happened, God cares. Whether we feel it or not, he is still our Father. His love never ends. And his purpose is that we should become like him, that we should share his character and his love. Through our sufferings we can, if we commit them to him and let him use them to correct and to train us.

## Sharing the sufferings of Christ

Time and again, when they deal with the problem of suffering, the New Testament writers encourage their readers to rejoice. 'My dear friends,' says the Apostle Peter, 'do not be surprised at the painful test you are suffering, as though something unusual were happening to you. Rather be glad ...' (1 Pet. 4: 12-13). Be glad, say the New Testament

123

writers, because you are sharing the sufferings of Christ.

This sharing in the sufferings of Christ is a priceless privilege, available only to the Christian. It is one way to knowing the power of Christ. It guarantees the Christian's future glory. 'All I want', says Paul, 'is to know Christ and to experience the power of his resurrection, to share in his sufferings and become like him in his death, in the hope that I myself will be raised from death to life' (Phil. 3: 10-11).

Sharing in Christ's sufferings equips the Christian to join God in helping others (2 Cor. 1: 5). In other words, until we have suffered ourselves, we cannot help others who are also suffering. Indeed, through our hard experiences we actually help Christ's body, the church, to endure the suffering which awaits it. 'By means of my physical sufferings', says Paul, 'I am helping to complete what still remains of Christ's sufferings on behalf of his body, the church' (Col. 1: 24).

How can there be anything left of Christ's sufferings? Surely, they are ended. Surely, he sits in power and glory and honour at his Father's right hand. Is he not waiting for his enemies to be made the footstool for his feet? (Heb. 1: 13). Is not his personal return in triumph promised on almost every page in the New Testament, the climax of human history, the certain dawn of an eternal morning, when righteousness will reign for evermore? How can Jesus still be suffering?

The personal sufferings of Jesus in his earthly life ended, of course, at the cross. He died, never to die again. In that sense, his sufferings have ended. In the same sense, Christ's sufferings for our salvation are also ended. Christ was offered once for all. He can never be put to death again, nor can his offering ever be repeated, nor can anyone ever have a share in Christ's offering for sin on the cross.

But the world is still Christ's world. He made it and he controls its course. And the world is still lost and in rebellion against him. Although Christ rules, the world is still in the power of the Evil One. Because sin is still present the world is a suffering world. Pain, sickness, exploitation, cruelty, bereavement and injustice are still the everyday human experience of millions of people around the world. Because Christ loves his world he still suffers on its behalf. He still weeps over Jerusalem. He is still filled with pity at the suffering in his world. And when Christians, like everyone else, are caught up in the world's suffering, they share in the sufferings of Christ. Christ suffers with them, and so they can rejoice.

Are you suffering from an incurable, debilitating illness? Do you know the pain of marriage breakdown and divorce? Are you mourning the loss of an infant child, or a close friend, or a lifelong partner? Do you feel ashamed, rejected and a failure because you are unemployed? Is life a desperate struggle to make ends meet on a low income with no prospects, while others relax in idle luxury? Then you are sharing in the sufferings of Christ. He is suffering with you. He knows your situation and condition better than you know it yourself. And he cares.

Christ also suffers when his church suffers. 'Saul, Saul! Why do you persecute me?' he asked (Acts 9: 4). When Saul tried to destroy the church, going from house to house in Jerusalem, dragging out the believers, both men and women, and throwing them into jail, it was Jesus he was attacking (Acts 8: 3).

In many parts of the world Christians still suffer torture and imprisonment because they are faithful to Jesus. But wherever people live unashamedly for him they will be scorned and ridiculed, slighted and misunderstood. Paul speaks of hardship and danger, sleeplessness and hunger, weariness and poverty gladly endured for the sake of Jesus Christ. For he knows that when Christians suffer like this they are sharing in the sufferings of Christ.

In the imprisonment of Christians in Siberia because they refuse to allow State-appointed leaders to control their church affairs, Christ is suffering. In the mental torture of believers in psychiatric hospitals in Eastern Europe because they dare to demand freedom of religious conviction against the all-embracing demands of atheistic, Marxist-Leninist philosophy, Christ is suffering. In the apathy which rejects the valiant efforts of Christians to present the Gospel in the selfish, affluent West, Christ is suffering. He suffers because the church is his body and he is its head. He suffers because, in all these things, Christians are sharing in his suffering.

Besides all this, Christians are called to a deeper level of sharing. The suffering we have discussed so far has been involuntary. The disappointments and tragedies of life come to us unexpectedly. Rejection by others because we belong to Jesus Christ is not something we actively seek. But Christ's sufferings were not involuntary. 'Of his own free will he gave up all he had ... and walked the path of obedience all the way to death – his death on the cross' (Phil. 2: 7, 8). Christ never had to suffer. He took it upon himself gladly for the world's salvation.

In the same way, Christ calls his followers to enter into suffering on his behalf. 'If anyone wants to come with me, he must forget self, carry his cross, and follow me' (Mark 8: 34). He calls us to share in his sufferings, as we enter into the world's sufferings with him.

In 1912 a young woman called Dorothy Kerin died. For most of her brief life she had suffered dreadfully from one kind of incurable illness after another. To those who stood round her bedside when her life expired, death seemed a merciful release. Twenty minutes after her heart had stopped beating, to the utter astonishment of all who were there, Dorothy showed signs of life. Soon she was breathing normally again and making a dramatic, miraculous recovery. With new life and new health she would live another fifty years.

Later, Dorothy described how, when she was dead, she heard a voice calling 'Will you go back?' She knew the voice was the voice of Jesus. 'Yes,' she had replied, 'I will go back.' Her new life became a walk with Jesus, in devotion and holiness, which inspired and challenged all who met her. So deeply did she live in him and he in her that, within five years, the five wounds of Christ's crucifixion, the stigmata, in hands, feet and side, had appeared in Dorothy's body. From them, she felt real pain. From them, she bled real blood.

They were seen by a number of honourable people at the time. Later, the wounds healed and became invisible, but Dorothy continued to feel pain from them for the rest of her life.

Dorothy also discovered that God had given her a quite remarkable ministry of healing. Many on whom she laid her hands recovered from various illnesses. Yet her ministry was not the ministry of a magician or faith healer. For with the healing ministry went a ministry of prayer. Dorothy learned in prayer to enter into the condition of those who were sick and, as she did, they were healed. With Christ, she shared their suffering and, as she did, they were made well.

Dorothy Kerin was unusual. Only a handful of Christians through the ages (Francis of Assisi, Padre Pio, for example) are known to have borne the stigmata. But Dorothy learned that ministry in the Name of Christ involves suffering with Christ, for his whole ministry was a ministry of suffering. Christ calls us to bring good news to the poor, and we can only do that as we learn to share their poverty. Christ calls us to set free the oppressed and we shall only do that as we enter into their oppression. Real service for Christ involves identifying with the world Christ came to save in all its lostness, injustice, poverty and oppression.

This is what Christians have always done and are still doing. They give up lucrative jobs with comfort and security in order to make Christ known. They cross the seven seas and struggle with difficult languages and cultural alienation to proclaim Jesus where his name is unheard. They risk debilitating illness, misunderstanding from fellow Christians, rejection of their message, opposition from friend and foe, all for the sake of Christ. With Jesus they share willingly in his sufferings.

This is what Paul means when he talks about completing what still remains of Christ's physical sufferings on behalf of his body, the church (Col. 1: 24). As long as the world and the church suffer, Christ suffers. And he calls us to share in the completion of his suffering. Are we willing to take up the cross and follow him?

'If you are insulted because you are Christ's followers,' says
the Apostle Peter, 'this means that the glorious Spirit, the
Spirit of God, is resting on you' (1 Pet. 4: 14). Here is another
reason why Christians can rejoice in suffering; it shows that
they are filled with the Holy Spirit.

Peter, have we read you right? Our suffering for Christ
means we are filled with the Spirit?

Yes, my children. You have read me right. That is exactly
what I mean.

But Peter, we always thought our spiritual gifts were the
evidence that we are filled with the Spirit. When we pray in
tongues. When we see people healed in the Name of Jesus.
When demons are cast out. When the Gospel is preached and
people are converted through the effective preaching of the
Gospel; we always thought that was the evidence that we are
filled with the Spirit. Now you say it is not like that at all.
What do you mean?

Come, come, my children! How forgetful you are! Do you
not remember what Jesus said about the spiritual gifts?
'When Judgement Day comes, many will say to me, "Lord,
Lord! In your name we spoke God's message, by your name
we drove out many demons and performed many miracles!"
Then I will say to them, "I never knew you. Get away from
me, you wicked people!"' (Matt. 7: 22-23). In themselves, the
spiritual gifts prove nothing, because every single one of
them can be copied by ourselves or by the Devil. Doing what
our Father in heaven wants is what really counts. And he
calls us to take up our cross and follow Jesus and suffer with
him.

We know that, Peter. Does that mean that the spiritual
gifts do not matter after all? Jesus also said, 'Believers will be
given the power to perform miracles: they will drive out
demons in my name; they will speak in ... tongues; if they
pick up snakes or drink any poison, they will not be harmed;
they will place their hands on sick people, who will get well'
(Mark 16: 17-18). And you: whenever we read about your

being filled with the Spirit you are exercising one or more of the spiritual gifts. Yet now you say they prove nothing.

Of course the spiritual gifts matter. Of course we should use them to the glory of Jesus and the strengthening of his church. But when we use them we must expect to suffer, and our suffering, rather than the gifts, will prove that the Spirit of God is resting on us. When I and the other disciples were filled with the Spirit on the Day of Pentecost we were scorned and ridiculed because people thought we were drunk. When John and I were filled with the Spirit in front of the Jewish Council we were warned never again to speak to anyone in the name of Jesus (Acts 4: 8-17). That was the proof of the Spirit. That was how we knew that Jesus was with us; when we were scorned and flogged and imprisoned for him.

Well all right, then, Peter. So the gifts are not that important after all. But what about our lives? We thought our lives were the proof that we are filled with the Spirit. When the fruit of the Spirit is seen in our lives, when love, joy, peace, patience, kindness, goodness, faithfulness, humility and self-control are displayed, then we know that the Spirit of God is resting on us. Is that not what Paul says in his letter to the Galatians?

Yes, of course, my children. Our lives are important too. But can you not see that all those fruits of the Spirit only demonstrate the Spirit when they are displayed in the context of suffering? Jesus told us that love, his love, is only seen when we love our enemies. Patience is only patience when we would normally be impatient. Joy is joy in suffering. Peace is the peace of Christ which passes knowledge when everything is falling all about us, and we know his calm and presence deep in our souls. You see, once again, it is as we suffer for him that we know that his Spirit is with us.

Do you not remember what Jesus said, '"No slave is greater than his master." If they persecuted me, they will persecute you too' (John 15: 20)? Because he is with us we suffer. Because people see Jesus in you and me they attack us as they attacked him. That is why our suffering proves that his Spirit is resting on us. That is why we have to be sure that when we suffer we are suffering for him, and not because we have done wrong ourselves.

*Bearing Christ's Name*

What is the most important thing in life – a home, good health, a wife or husband, a family, a good job, security for the future? The apostle Peter says the most important and precious thing in life is to bear Christ's name (1 Pet. 4: 16). Belonging to Jesus, growing in his family, obeying and serving him; these things matter more than anything else. 'The Kingdom of heaven is like treasure hidden in a field, which a man found and covered up; then in his joy he goes and sells all that he has and buys that field' (Matt. 13: 44 RSV). We can lose everything we may have in life, including life itself, but we can never lose Jesus. He is ours for always. Therefore, however cruel life seems to be, whatever we may have to suffer because, directly or indirectly, we belong to Jesus, we can thank God that we bear Christ's name.

Christians live in a world under judgment because it has lost its way and rebelled against God. They are not exempt from the judgment and the suffering which goes with it. But the purpose of the judgment is different. God's judgment on the world serves as a constant reminder of his presence and power. God's judgment on the church is designed to strengthen its faith in him and in his loving care. 'So then, those who suffer because it is God's will for them, should by their good actions trust themselves completely to their Creator, who always keeps his promise' (1 Pet. 4: 19).

Thirty-five years ago Geoffrey Bull went as a young missionary to Tibet. While he was there Mao Tse-Tung came to power in neighbouring China. Soon, his Communist army had overrun Tibet and Geoffrey was arrested and imprisoned. For over two years he was brainwashed, mentally and physically tortured in an attempt to destroy his faith in Christ. Towards the end, as he neared breaking-point he made an amazing discovery. What mattered was no longer his hold on Christ, but Christ's hold on him. Geoffrey might fail, but Jesus never would. Through Christ, and his strength, he survived.

Rejoicing in suffering is the most unnatural thing in the world. Of ourselves, we can never do it. But with Christ we can, because we suffer for him, and with him, on behalf of his body, the church. If we share his sufferings, we shall also share his resurrection.

# CHAPTER 11 – THE FAMILY SPIRIT

Scattered around the countryside in all their solitary splendour stand the stately homes of England: Chatsworth House, Kedleston Hall, Blenheim Palace, and the like. Each has been passed down from father to son over many generations. Successive owners have extended and improved the homes and gardens and developed the surrounding estates. Behind these 'family firms' has been a spirit of responsibilities over hundreds of years. Without that spirit the families' wealth would have been dissipated and their estates destroyed.

A Spirit inspires the family of God too; not some vague, indefinable tradition as in the aristocratic families of the landed gentry, but a living reality who guides and controls all Christians individually and in their life together. He is the Spirit of the living God. We have spoken of him frequently in this book. Now we draw the threads together for 'Whoever does not have the Spirit of Christ does not belong to him' (Rom. 8: 9).

## The Holy Spirit is personal

Often in the Bible the Holy Spirit is compared to an impersonal influence, such as wind, fire, oil, etc. But when Jesus teaches about the Holy Spirit he always uses the personal pronoun: *He* reveals the truth about God. The world cannot receive *him*, because it cannot see *him* or know *him*. But you know *him*, because *he* remains with you and is in you (John 14: 17).

We cannot know an influence, but we can know a person. Just as we can know God as a loving father, and Christ as his Son, so we can know the Holy Spirit in a living, personal way.

## The Holy Spirit is eternal

The very first scene in the Bible story shows the Holy Spirit at work in the making of the world; 'the Spirit of God was moving over the face of the waters' (Gen. 1: 2 RSV). The Holy Spirit is a part of the Godhead. It is impossible to say 'God' with true biblical meaning without saying 'Father', 'Son' and 'Holy Spirit'. Many Scriptures speak of the Eternal God in such terms (for example, Matt. 28: 19; 2 Cor. 13: 13; Heb. 9: 14).

## The Holy Spirit brings us into the family of God

Our first dawning interest in Christian living is prompted by the Holy Spirit. This is more than a new hobby, a girl-friend's persuasions or the impression made by an eloquent preacher. He is at work. He makes us dissatisfied with ourselves. He convinces us of our sin, he shows us what is right, he warns us of coming judgment. He brings us to know and understand the love of God in Jesus and he implants new life in our hearts enabling us to believe in Christ and put our trust in him. 'A person is born physically of human parents, but he is born spiritually of the Spirit' (John 3: 6). 'No one can enter the Kingdom of God unless he is born of water and the Spirit' (John 3: 5).

## The Holy Spirit makes us like Jesus

As we showed in chapter seven, God's purpose in bringing us into his family is to make us 'like his Son' (Rom. 8: 29). This is the work of the Holy Spirit. By ourselves we cannot do it. If we try to be good, we fail. But throughout our earthly lifetime the Spirit begins to make us like Jesus. He gives us power to break compulsive habits of speech and behaviour. He heals our inner wounds which make us behave irrationally and harmfully. And as we walk with Jesus and allow the Spirit to rule our lives he produces all the elements of Christian character we need so much. 'The Spirit produces love, joy, peace, patience, kindness, goodness, faithfulness, humility, and self-control ... The Spirit has given us life; he must also control our lives' Gal. 5: 22-25).

## The Holy Spirit enables us to worship God

When the woman at the well tried to engage Jesus in a religious argument about the proper place to worship God, Jesus replied, 'God is Spirit, and only by the power of his Spirit can people worship him as he really is' (John 4: 24). The Spirit enables us to worship God on our own. He prays for us with sighs too deep for words (Rom. 8: 26). Through the gift of tongues he enables us to pray in our spirits to God (1 Cor. 14: 2). In reverent silence, joyful singing or praying aloud in words of our own choice or taken from books; in all of these exercises, he inspires our private devotions.

The same Spirit enables us to take a genuine part in corporate worship, when we gather with other Christians in church congregations or small groups. He gives to one person a hymn, another a teaching, another a revelation from God, another a message in tongues, and still another the explanation of what is said (1 Cor. 14: 26).

All Christian worship has two elements: a set form and the spontaneous expression of the Spirit. When Christians abandon one set form they always invent another. The set forms can be arid and dry or they can throb with life. All set forms should allow some room for the free operation of the Spirit. When the Spirit is active in the hearts of worshipping people then both the set forms and the spontaneous contributions of the worshippers enable God's family to worship him as he really is.

### The Holy Spirit equips us for Christian service

We can only witness for Christ and work in the family firm as the Holy Spirit directs us and equips us. If we try in our own strength our message will fall on deaf ears and all our best efforts will come to nothing. But the Holy Spirit pours out gifts for Christian service. To one person he gives a message full of wisdom and to another a message full of knowledge. To others he gives faith, the power to heal, the power to work miracles and the ability to speak God's message. Others can distinguish between gifts that come from the Spirit and those that do not. Yet others have the particular gift of bringing messages in tongues and others are able to explain what is said. All these gifts come from the same Spirit, to strengthen the church and enable it to grow (1 Cor. 12: 4-11).

Other gifts of the Spirit are given to particular individuals, enabling them to hold recognised positions of ministry and leadership in the church. So Paul describes those who are appointed to be apostles, prophets, evangelists, pastors and teachers. Again, the purpose is to prepare all God's people for the work of Christian service, in order to build up the body of Christ (Eph. 4: 11-12). Some Christians are enabled to live sacrificially in a financial way for Christ, while to others is given the grace to lay down their lives for him (1 Cor. 13: 3). Yet others receive particular strength not to marry for many years or even a lifetime in order to devote themselves wholeheartedly to Christian service (1 Cor. 7: 1-7, 32-5). All these gifts come from the Holy Spirit to make our service for Christ effective.

Different Christians receive different gifts. They should not boast about their gifts, nor should they be envious of the gifts of others. For the Spirit distributes his gifts 'as he wishes' (1 Cor. 12: 11). Different gifts enable the Christian family to function as a body with different members all contributing to the smooth working of the whole. Therefore, with their different gifts all Christians need each other. We are not all called to be big-name Christians with international ministries, nor can the well known and famous manage without the humble contributions of their seemingly insignificant brothers and sisters.

So we should rejoice in our gifts. We should set our hearts on them, but we should always remember that without love our gifts will be noisy and discordant and will bring dishonour on the name of Jesus. One day, the gifts will be withdrawn, but love, for Christ and for each other, will last for ever (1 Cor. 13).


## The Holy Spirit guarantees our future

A glorious future awaits the Christian. He is promised all the joys of heaven for ever. But the promise is not merely 'pie in the sky when you die'. Whoever has the Son has eternal life now (1 John 5: 11-12). Already he is beginning to enjoy the blessings of heaven. This privilege is his through the Holy Spirit. 'The Spirit is the guarantee that we shall receive what God has promised his people' (Eph. 1: 14).

Economically, we live increasingly in a credit-based society. More and more we buy things, not with cash, but on the never-never. When we make such purchases, of a house, a car, some furniture, or anything else, we make a down-payment. That is the guarantee to the seller that we shall make the remaining payments on time until we have paid fully. When Paul says that the Spirit is the guarantee that we shall recieve what God has promised, he used a word which carries the idea of 'first instalment' of heaven.

Sometimes, when we buy on the never-never, we fail to keep up with the payments. Then what we have bought is reclaimed by the seller and we are worse off then we were before. But God never fails to make his payments. He never withdraws or withholds his promise of heaven. 'God, who began this good work in you, will carry it on until it is finished on the Day of Christ Jesus' (Phil. 1: 6).

As we walk in the Spirit, so God gives us more of heaven. As we worship in the Spirit so we are united on earth with the church triumphant in heaven; 'with angels and archangels and all the company of heaven we laud and magnify your glorious name, evermore praising you.' We do not earn our way to heaven. God gives it to us as he gives us every other spiritual blessing in Christ. And through the Holy Spirit he guarantees that we shall receive what he has promised.

## Receiving the Holy Spirit

Bilquis Sheikh was an aristocratic Muslim lady living in ample, financial security if rural Pakistan. Through an amazing series of events, some natural and some supernatural, God broke into her life and brought her to a living faith in Christ. As he did so, she had to experience God as Father, as Son and as Holy Spirit before her new-found faith was complete (Bilquis Sheikh, *I Dared to Call Him Father*). Bilquis Sheikh's experience illustrates and clarifies a dilemma which has often beset Western Christians. They are happy to call God, 'our Father'. They are happy to believe on the Lord Jesus Christ to be saved. But somehow they are not very sure where the Holy Spirit fits in.

Often, the Holy Spirit is neglected altogether. Apart from formal inclusion in blessings and that kind of thing, sincere and devout Christians may live for years without any practical understanding of the Holy Spirit. Frequently their lives are impoverished and powerless as a result.

Sometimes Christians have assumed that because they have received Christ they have automatically received the Holy Spirit as well. After all, does not Paul say, 'Whoever does not have the Spirit of Christ does not belong to him' (Rom. 8: 9)? If we cannot have Christ without his Spirit, why worry too much about the Holy Spirit once we have put our trust in Jesus. This approach has much to commend it. God does give us his Spirit when we believe in Jesus. The only problem is that, for all practical purposes, Christians in this group often end up like the ones in the first group. Although they pay lip-service to the Holy Spirit they are often largely ignorant of him as a living reality in their lives. When they meet Christians for whom the Spirit is real, they sometimes feel threatened and defensive as a result.

In their desire to give the Holy Spirit a proper place in their experience, yet other Christians have sometimes tacked him on to their faith in Christ as a sort of necessary extra. First, they say, we believe in Christ for salvation and then, some time later, we receive or are baptised in the Holy Spirit. While this approach certainly ensures that the Holy Spirit is not neglected there are intrinsic dangers in it. It can detract from the sufficiency of the work of Christ on our behalf. Receiving the Holy Spirit becomes something extra to faith in Christ. Before long we are welcoming people, not because they believe in Jesus, but because they have received his Spirit. The ground of our salvation has been subtly shifted.

We must not stereotype Christian experience. Some Christians, like the Samaritans, do consciously trust Christ for salvation, and then receive the Spirit later (Acts 8: 4-17). Some, like Saul on the Damascus road, do have an overwhelming experience of Christ, which is followed later by infilling with the Holy Spirit (Acts 9: 1-19). But with other Christians the order happens the other way round. The Gentiles at Caesarea were filled with the Holy Spirit and then expressed their faith in Christ in baptism (Acts 10: 44-8). Many different Christians have many different experiences of the Holy Spirit. Christian experience is as varied as human nature itself. Certainly there is no single stereotyped experience described or taught in the New Testament. Attempts to prove that there is can only be bolstered by overemphasising some Scriptures and ignoring others.

In his Pentecostal sermon Peter makes it clear that reception of the Holy Spirit is an expected consequence of repentance, baptism and faith for forgiveness (Acts 2: 38). Knowing God as Father, finding salvation in Christ and

139

receiving the Holy Spirit are all part of the 'package deal' God gives when we trust in Jesus. Sometimes when we open the package we receive all the elements at once. Sometimes there is a separation between them in time. When that happens we should look for the elements of the package we have missed. Acts 8 tells us of such a situation. Whatever the cause, Peter and John were so concerned that they travelled from Jerusalem to Samaria. There 'they prayed for the believers that they might receive the Holy Spirit ... Then Peter and John placed their hands on them and they received the Holy Spirit' (vv. 15-17).

Have you received the Holy Spirit? Certainly if you are a Christian at all, he lives within you. But have you consciously welcomed him? Have you trusted him to fill you, as you have trusted Christ to save you? Do you know something of his power to change your old life and to sustain your new one? Perhaps, because you have never been properly taught, your Christian life is lacking in this area. Then receive the Holy Spirit now.

You can receive the Holy Spirit simply by asking him into your life. 'Bad as you are,' said Jesus, 'you know how to give good things to your children. How much more, then, will the Father in heaven give the Holy Spirit to those who ask him!' (Luke 11: 13). When you have asked the Spirit to come in, believe that you have received him, and begin to praise God for what he has done. Do not be surprised if your praise results in your speaking in tongues; it does not have to, but it is quite likely! If you receive this gift of prayer in language then begin to use it regularly along with your other prayers.

Maybe you are frightened of receiving the Holy Spirit. That is quite natural. When we read some of the staggering things the first Christians did when they were filled with the Spirit, and some of the appalling suffering they endured as a result, we are likely to be afraid of similar things happening to us. Perhaps you are afraid of receiving the Spirit's gifts. Maybe you have heard wild stories or had disturbing experiences of people supposedly under the influence of the

Holy Spirit. Will that happen to you? Will you become a religious maniac?

The Holy Spirit is given by a loving Father. He does not give bad things to his children, but good things. We need not be afraid of the Holy Spirit, for with the Spirit comes all the strength and grace we need to face what God has for us.

Maybe you have asked the Spirit into your life and nothing has seemingly happened. You are still defeated and frustrated as you were before. Another way to receive the Spirit is through the laying-on-of-hands by one or more fellow Christians. Search out a friend or minister whom you know is filled with the Spirit. Ask him or her to pray with you that you might receive the Spirit too. Go to a renewal meeting or a festival of praise where ministry in the Spirit is given. Respond to the invitation at the end of the meeting that others might pray with you there. Once you have asked, believe that you have received and begin to act accordingly. 'Everyone who asks will receive, and he who seeks will find, and the door will be opened to anyone who knocks' (Luke 11: 10).

## Being filled with the Holy Spirit

We only receive Christ for salvation, once. There is only one beginning to our new life in the family of God. But we can receive the Holy Spirit again and again. When we walk in the Spirit each day, God will sometimes fill us with his Spirit in order to enable us to meet a special need or crisis. This happened often in the New Testament, and we can expect it to happen to us, too.

When Peter and John were first arrested and called before the Jewish Council to explain how the lame man at the Beautiful Gate of the Temple had been healed, 'Peter, full of the Holy Spirit, answered them' (Acts 4: 8). When Stephen was stopped in mid-speech by the angry members of the same Council who could not bear to hear his message of

141

judgment, full of the Holy Spirit he looked up to heaven and saw God's glory (Acts 7: 55).

All through our lives, we can keep on asking for the fullness of God's Spirit to equip us for the situations we know we shall meet. This, in fact, is what the New Testament tells us to do. 'Do not get drunk with wine, which will only ruin you;' warns Paul, 'instead, be filled with the Spirit' (Eph. 5: 18). The verb Paul uses has a continuous meaning: 'go on being filled with the Spirit,' he says.

Too many Christians look back to an experience of the Spirit years ago and imagine they have received all that God has for them. But God wants us to grow in the Spirit, to walk in the Spirit, to become mature people, reaching to the very height of Christ's full stature. In this we shall often fail. There will be many setbacks. We shall grieve and quench the Spirit by our stubborn attitudes and our disobedience to Christ's commands. But we can always come back. We can receive the Spirit again when we have failed him. The Family Spirit, who has filled and inspired our Christian brothers for 2,000 years can fill and inspire us and enable us to live to Christ's glory, now, and in the world to come.

# CHAPTER 12 – THE FAMILY FORTUNE

Ernie was a dustman in the south of England. Day after day, he wore himself out carrying people's rubbish to the dustcart and emptying it at the refuse disposal plant. He lived modestly with his wife and family, enjoyed an annual holiday and looked forward to retirement and release from the exacting demands of his wearisome work. One morning, to his total surprise, he received a letter from an unknown solicitor. A distant and unheard-of relative had died, leaving extensive lands and a vast fortune. Ernie had been traced as the nearest surviving heir. In one moment, Ernie the dustman had become a titled member of the aristocracy. The subsequent transformation in his way of life was total. Financial anxiety was gone for good. All that he had ever wanted for himself and his family was now available. He never emptied another dustbin, but learned instead the intricacies of high finance and estate management.

Few people ever enjoy an experience like Ernie's. Some can look forward to a substantial inheritance. For most, receiving a legacy is a distant dream, only experienced vicariously in the pages, perhaps, of a romantic novel. But for every Christian there is an inheritance far richer, more enduring and more satisfying than Ernie's ever was. 'We have been born anew to ... an inheritance which is imperishable, undefiled, and unfading, kept in heaven' (1 Pet. 1: 3, 4 RSV).

The Christian hope of future glory has often been scorned and derided as 'pie in the sky when you die', a means of escape from the pressing problems of the world around us, an excuse for inaction in the face of poverty, injustice and oppression. In fact, those who have achieved the most positive and lasting good for this world have always been those who have had their sights set most clearly on the next.

Without a future hope, any faith and any way of life becomes meaningless and a sham. A Marxist was heckling a Christian preacher on Liverpool pierhead. 'Pie in the sky when you die! Pie in the sky when you die!' he chanted. So the preacher stopped and asked the heckler to what he was looking forward. Enthusiastically, the Marxist pointed to a society of economic equality wherein each would work according to his means and each would receive according to his needs. The end of exploitation would spell the end of lawlessness and crime. All would live in peace and plenty for evermore. 'Pie in the sky when you die?' replied the preacher. 'That sounds to me like cake on the slate if you wait!'

Unlike the Marxist hope which continually recedes into an ever more distant future, the Christian hope is sure and certain. And in finding its fulfilment in the next world it is totally realistic. For there are always limits to the possibilities of a world out of step with God. There are even limits to what the Gospel can do in a world of unbelief. In Nazareth, Jesus found he could do little, 'because the people did not have faith' (Mark 6: 6).

Christians talk of peace and joy and a sense of purpose in this life, and rightly so. But what happens at the hospital when the consultant tells you he can do no more? What do you do when the secret police knock on your door at two in the morning, when discipleship costs far more than it gives, when you are beginning to fall in love with another man's wife and know you must never see her again, when the person nearest and dearest to you dies, when the word 'No' is the bitterest and hardest in your vocabulary?

Peter and Paul wrote about the Christian inheritance to readers who were despised by their neighbours and regarded as 'a class hated for their abominations'. Some of them would live to see their wives pushed into the arena to be gored by bulls and clawed by lions. They themselves would be nailed to posts, covered in pitch and set on fire to provide lamps for entertainment. To *them* Peter wrote, 'My dear friends, do not be surprised at the painful test you are suffering, as though something unusual were happening to you. Rather be glad that you are sharing Christ's sufferings, so that you may be full of joy when his glory is revealed' (1 Pet. 4: 12-13). Paul encouraged *them* to believe they were 'heirs of God and fellow heirs with Christ, provided we suffer with him in order that we may also be glorified with him' (Rom. 8: 17 RSV).

Without an inheritance the Christian life is a mockery. Without a positive future our faith becomes slick and superficial. For every prayer is not answered the way we want it to be. Every 'claiming by faith' does not obtain what it claims. Every sickness is not cured. Every problem does not have an instant solution. The occasional travelling religious road-show may tell us otherwise, but the facts are different. 'If our hope in Christ is good for this life only and no more, then we deserve more pity than anyone else in all the world' (1 Cor. 15: 19).

What, then, is the Christian hope? What is the inheritance, guaranteed by the Holy Spirit, and reserved for us in heaven?


*Our bodies will be changed*

In our present bodies we 'groan within ourselves, as we wait for God to make us his sons and set our whole being free' (Rom. 8: 23). No wonder we groan! Our bodies wear out, let us down, hurt us and limit us. Being physical they are subject to chemical changes which affect our temperament, our feelings, our emotions, our health. Worst of all, they trap us into becoming servants of sin. Hands betray us into violence, lips into lies, ears into the hearing of evil, sexual organs into immorality. Not that it is bad or demeaning to have a body. Christ came in a body. The Holy Spirit makes temples of our bodies. But they constitute our weakest and most vulnerable doorway into wrongdoing.

In heaven, however, our bodies will be changed. From

being mortal, they will become immortal, and we shall live, never to die again. From being ugly, they will become beautiful. From being physical, they will become spiritual. At the moment, life in our bodies is like the life of a seed. In heaven, our dull, drab, unattractive seed-like lives will flower into the lives of full-grown plants.

Our example in all this is none other than the Lord Jesus himself. He took a body like ours with all its limitations. But one day he was changed. Peter, James and John saw him as he really was, shining, white, glorious (Mark 9: 2-8). Then he returned again to his earthly body. He accepted the pain, shame and humiliation of crucifixion and death. But he was raised. His body was changed. He still had a body which could eat, talk and be touched, but it was different. It could appear and disappear. It could pass through closed doors. It could ascend into the Father's presence for evermore.

'Just as we wear the likeness of [Adam] the man made of earth, so we will wear the likeness of the Man from heaven' (1 Cor. 15: 49). 'We eagerly wait for our Saviour, the Lord Jesus Christ, to come from heaven. He will change our weak mortal bodies and make them like his own glorious body' (Phil. 3: 20-21).


## Our minds will be enlarged

Not only our bodies but our minds are limited by our present mortality. There are truths and concepts we can never grasp. There are questions we can never answer, problems we can never solve. 'What I know now is only partial; then it will be complete – as complete as God's knowledge of me' (1 Cor. 13: 12).

Then the eternal mystery of the threefold Godhead will be revealed. Then the age-old problem of the presence of evil in a good world created and controlled by a good God will be solved. Then we shall understand how Jesus of Nazareth was at once fully human and fully divine. Then the endless questions surrounding God's free choice of us to be his children and our free response to his love will fall into place. Then we shall know how the world was made by God, how natural processes played their part in its formation, how life appeared and how the human race began. Then we shall understand the place of planet Earth in the mighty vastness of the universe. For through the Son, God has decided to bring the whole universe back to himself (Col. 1: 20). Nothing will elude us. Nothing will be too hard for us to understand.

*Our relationships will be transformed*

One of the seemingly strangest things Jesus says about heaven is that when the dead rise to life they will be like the angels and will not marry (Mark 12: 25). To someone parted by death from a lifetime's marriage, and longing to be reunited with the loved one, that seems a bleak prospect indeed, yet it lies at the heart of a true understanding of what heaven will be like. Jesus said it in response to a hypothetical story of a woman who had been married seven times! 'When all the dead rise to life ... whose wife will she be?' (Mark 12: 23).

Jesus was not denying that we shall be united with our loved ones when we die; if they have died in the faith of Christ we certainly shall. Nor was he painting a dismal picture of a super-spiritual existence in which all the choicest joys of earth will be denied. Jesus could only be implying that we shall there enjoy the kind of close, loving relationship with everyone that we enjoy with our married partners when our marriages are at their best. Mutual hostility and suspicion between people will end. Backbiting, jealousy and envy will be no more. Loneliness will be swept away. We shall belong to each other and rejoice in our mutual belonging.

Not only will our relationships with each other be transformed. Broken relationships between different groups of Christians will be renewed. Depending on your pet

147

denominational hate, a story is told of a group of newly-arrived Christians being shown around heaven. Each successive part of the celestial Kingdom thrilled and excited them more and more until they saw a group of people sitting together in an idyllic woodland glade. 'Who are those people?' one of the Christians asked their guiding angel. 'They're the Plymouth Brethren (or the Roman Catholics, or the Strict Baptists, or the Primitive Methodists or whatever), came the reply. 'You have to be very quiet. They don't know we're here!'

But we shall know the others are there. No matter how exclusive our denominational label on earth we shall meet together with all Christians around the throne of God and of the Lamb in Heaven. Christ will 'present the church to himself in all its beauty – pure and faultless, without spot or wrinkle or any other imperfection' (Eph. 5: 27). All the deep wounds in the body of Christ will be healed. All the bitter quarrels which have divided the family of God will be settled. All the hurtful memories will be forgiven. Christ will be all and in all, and the church will reflect his beauty.

International relationships will be transformed. Down the middle of the heavenly city's street flows the river of the water of life, coming from the throne of God and the Lamb. On each side of the river stands the tree of life bearing fruit each month, 'and its leaves are for the healing of the nations' (Rev. 22: 1-2). The sun and the moon do not shine in heaven because the glory of God shines there and the Lamb is its lamp. The peoples of the world walk by its light and the kings of the earth bring their wealth there (Rev. 21: 23-24). Divisions of race, culture, language and national boundaries will be ended. Righteousness will rule the world as God always intended.


## Our worship will be enriched

One of the most frequent pictures in the Book of Revelation with its glimpses into heaven is of angels and people worshipping God. This seems to be their constant activity. They cast their crowns before his throne and proclaim his eternal worth. They rejoice with endless thanksgiving at the salvation purchased by Christ at the cross. Nor is their worship confined by time and space. 'I did not see a temple in the city,' says John, 'because its temple is the Lord God Almighty and the Lamb' (Rev. 21: 22).

Gone will be dull services and the vicar's dreary sermons! Gone will be archaic and artificial language and music so often deemed necessary for Christian worship and praise. Worship will stem from full hearts, a never-ending, genuine expression of love for and thankfulness to Christ.

### Our environment will be perfected

Christians will not be alone in heaven. God's plan is to bring the whole universe back to himself (Col. 1: 20). All of creation waits with eager longing for God to reveal his sons. Then it will be set free from its slavery to pain and decay to share the glorious freedom of the children of God (Rom. 8: 19-22).

Some Christians have sometimes talked a lot of sentimental nonsense about being reunited with their pets in heaven. But animals will be there, as they are part of God's creation. And the animals too will be transformed in their relationship with each other and with us.

> Wolves and sheep will live together in peace,
> and leopards will lie down with young goats.
> Calves and lion cubs will feed together,
> and little children will take care of them.
> Cows and bears will eat together,
> and their calves and cubs will lie down in peace.
> Lions will eat straw as cattle do.
> Even a baby will not be harmed if it plays near a
> poisonous snake (Isa. 11: 6-8).

We have never been more conscious of the threat to our environment than we are today. Whole species of animals are being slaughtered to extinction through man's greed for their products. Vast areas of natural beauty are being sacrificed to man's lust for mineral extraction and the wealth which goes with it. The delicate balance of nature is in danger of being irreparably destroyed by industrial pollution. Nuclear war threatens to destroy human civilisation.

In heaven we shall live in a perfect environment. God's creation will flourish according to his original intention. Beauty, peace and plenty will be its hallmarks. And in its glorious, renewed state, God's creation will last for ever.

## Evil and all its consequences will be banished

In heaven there will be no more pain. Hunger, thirst and torture will end. God will wipe away every tear from our eyes (Rev. 7: 16-17). These things will have gone for good because evil will have been destroyed. Satan will be thrown into the lake of fire (Rev. 20: 10). The arch-enemy of Christ will never tempt and trouble us again.

Evil people will be excluded from heaven. The Bible writers may look forward to the restoration of the universe and the glorification of the church but they never include everyone in the Christian's future hope. 'Nothing that is impure will enter the city, nor anyone who does shameful things or tells lies' (Rev. 21: 27). 'Outside the city are the perverts and those who practise magic, the immoral and the murderers, those who worship idols and those who are liars both in words and deeds' (Rev. 22: 15).

How could it be otherwise? How could those who have forsaken and rejected Christ all their earthly lives, suddenly be happily integrated into his eternal kingdom where righteousness dwells? If everyone everywhere will ultimately go to heaven, whatever their manner of life on earth, what is the point in following Christ? Why proclaim him to others? Why endure hardship and danger, taking the Gospel to remote tribes in the four corners of the earth if those tribespeople will find their way to heaven anyway?

The idea of people heading for a lost eternity may not be popular or pleasant, but the fact remains that the Christian hope is for Christians. If it were otherwise it would not be the Christian hope. 'Only those whose names are written in the Lamb's book of the living will enter the city' (Rev. 21: 27).

We do not work our way to heaven. We do not earn it through good deeds or religious behaviour. Those who are there are those who have washed their robes and made them white with the blood of the Lamb. That is why they stand before God's throne and serve him day and night in his temple (Rev. 7: 14-15). And that is why we shall join them. We have been born into the family of God. We have been forgiven at the foot of the cross. We have been filled with the Holy Spirit and placed as living members within the body of Christ which is his church. And none of this has happened to us because we have deserved it or earned it. In his grace God has loved us, brought us into his family and will bring us into his eternal kingdom.

## We shall see Christ and be like him

This is the most thrilling part of the family fortune, to see Jesus for ourselves and to be like him. Mr Standfast, one of John Bunyan's characters in *Pilgrim's Progress*, says as he crosses the river of death, 'I see myself now at the end of my journey: my toilsome days are ended. I am going to see that head that was crowned with thorns and that face that was spit upon for me. I have formerly lived by hearsay and faith; but now I go where I shall live by sight and shall be with him in whose company I shall delight myself.'

A young sailor came home from HMS *Hermes* and the Falklands Campaign. Flags were hung all over his house. Bunting was stretched across the street. A table was laid on the pavement. Food was served and wine was prepared. Friends, relatives and neighbours gathered from near and far. As his car rounded the corner, music was played, 'Welcome home!'

It will be something like that, only far more wonderful when we arrive in heaven. Jesus, our Elder Brother, will be waiting to greet us. 'Well done, you good and faithful servant!...Come on in and share my happiness!' (Matt. 25: 23). Saints and angels will be gathered round. A whole new dimension of living will lie before us.

'My dear friends, we are now God's children, but it is not yet clear what we shall become. But we know that when Christ appears, we shall be like him, because we shall see him as he really is. Everyone who has this hope in Christ keeps himself pure just as Christ is pure' (1 John 3: 2-3).

# POSTSCRIPT – HOW TO BE BORN AGAIN

Perhaps you began to read this book, thinking you were a Christian.

'I believe in God – somebody must have made us.'

'The church is a good thing, and I go every Christmas and Easter.'

'Yes, of course I'm a Christian – where do you think I was born'

– the middle of Africa?'

'A Christian? Well I suppose so – I was christened, wasn't I?'

Thousands of people think like this, but for them God has no personal reality, prayer is no more than a cry in the dark and worship is a mere weekly duty. The Bible is a book of conundrums, and talk about Jesus is slightly embarrassing.

Some people come to vital Christianity through a groping sense that there must be something more. Others arrive because they hear the truth of the Gospel frankly and forcefully presented. Others reach the truth because the kind of picture of Christian living which is described here suddenly strikes them as way beyond their own experience. 'If *this* is Christianity' (they begin to feel) 'then what *I* have is a good deal less!'

'I always assumed that I was a Christian because my parents went to church fairly often,' confessed eighteen-year-old Cheryl. 'Then when I heard a series of sermons on what it means to be a child of God, I got a real shock. Each week I felt like someone outside a warm lighted house, peering through one of the windows from the cold and dark outside. I wanted, more than anything, to get inside.'

'I used to think Christianity was simply a life of decency and duty. People who spoke of having personal faith were odd people who were able to take a jump in the dark. Then quite suddenly I saw it in reverse. *I* was in the dark. What I had to do was step into the light.' So explained a university student to the visiting Christian Union speaker.

Ben was a burly factory-worker with no time for God. Like most of his mates he cracked that if he ever went inside a church, the roof would fall in on him. One day he ventured inside and that is (metaphorically) what happened. It was Easter Sunday, and his wife persuaded him to try it. He was thunderstruck at everything he saw: the crowded pews, the people pouring in and greeting each other noisily, the full-throated hymns and responses, the presence of every age group from teenagers in jeans to pensioners in dark suits, the sermon from a preacher brimming with joy and confidence. 'There is something here which I can't fathom. I'll give it three months' trial,' he said to his wife. The three months were soon forgotten, and a whole family became Christian – members of a greater Family.

Each of these people came by varied routes to the new birth. Every day someone, somewhere, is making a similar discovery.

*How can I be born again?*

As with human birth, there is no set pattern – no mechanical steps of 'one', 'two' and 'three'. Jane and John's baby (Chapter One) was born in the maternity home after a few hours' labour. Other parents will tell different stories involving in various combinations; doctors, nurses and midwives, hospital or home, brief pain or weeks of illness. Doctors will variously describe induced birth, the help of drugs, the usefulness of exercises, caesarian operations, and a variety of other means. The details differ; the principles remain the same.

So it is with the new birth. Jesus said it would be so. God is

154

the giver of life, and he reserves the right to work in a variety of ways. The wind is totally unpredictable and does not blow where we want it to. 'It is like that with everyone who is born of the Spirit' (John 3: 8).

Some people describe a sudden, almost violent conversion. Saul of Tarsus was like that – he who became Paul the Apostle. Interestingly, he described himself as 'someone whose birth was abnormal' (1 Cor. 15: 8). Others trace a period through which they came to eventual certainty and faith. Others again cannot recall when they were *reborn* but can describe vividly how they *came to be sure* (which is not quite the same thing). With some, the change is marked and decisive, but with others it comes only slowly and painfully, even after a time of decisive commitment.

When we think about the new birth we must always begin with God. We have to. A child does not choose to be born, does not conceive itself, does not bring itself to birth. So in the new birth, God acts first. 'Some did receive him and believed in him; so he gave them the right to become God's children. They did not become God's children by natural means, that is, by being born as the children of a human father; God himself was their Father' (John 1: 12-13).

God does not ask our permission and is not grateful when we comply with his wishes. 'God, I need to know. Show me, or I cannot see it. Do it for me, because I can do nothing for myself' – this is how we must come.


*How does God do it?*

When God brings us to new birth, he always uses the same means in various combinations.

*1 Truth from the Bible.* 'Faith comes from hearing the message' (Rom. 10: 17). Through the Bible God speaks. So read it regularly and humbly. One of two things will happen. Either it will convince you and faith will begin to dawn, or it will irritate and repel you, thus uncovering your true attitude to God.

The Gospel of John is specially and specifically written for this purpose. As you read, you are required to give a verdict. 'These (Gospel stories) have been written in order that you may believe that Jesus is the Son of God, and that through your faith in him you may have life' (John 20: 31).

2 *Power through the resurrection.* 'He gave us new life by raising Jesus Christ from death' (1 Pet. 1: 3). The new birth involves nothing less than a personal encounter with Jesus Christ. He died a horrible death almost 2,000 years ago – but within three days he was alive again, meeting his first disciples, explaining why his death had been necessary, and sending them with the Good News to the whole of mankind (Luke 24: 36-49). His death was the only means by which our sin and guilt could be forgiven. The resurrection that followed was the sign that its purpose was achieved. We could say that the cross was the paying of our debt and the resurrection was God's signing of the receipt!

## The response you must make

All this does not mean that you have no part to play. God deals with living people, not robots or puppets. He commands and invites our co-operation. We must repent. We must face the unpalatable facts of our wrong relationship with God and our faulty thoughts, words and deeds. Then we must change our direction. 'Repent and turn to God, so that he will forgive your sins,' we are told (Acts 3: 19).

*We must believe and trust in Christ.* 'No one can please God without faith' (Heb. 11: 6). Faith does *not* mean 'believing what you know isn't true', as the schoolboy howler defined. Quite simply, we take God at his word. We trust Jesus to bring us to the Father. We can pray a simple prayer.

God I have listened to what you say in the Bible. I admit

my guilt, my shame, my emptiness and my need. Thank you for the provisions you have made for me in Jesus. Please give me the new life which you promise to those who trust you. Take away my sin, and help me to live a life that pleases you.

*We must make an open witness.* 'If you confess that Jesus is Lord and believe that God raised him from death, you will be saved' (Rom. 10: 9). Find someone who will understand, and share your new determination and commitment. You are not alone. You belong to the Family. And the Father will never leave you.

# Donald Bridge and David Phypers

# THE MEAL THAT UNITES?

*An indispensable introduction to the Eucharist or Lord's Supper*

Bread and wine are at the heart of Christian worship. Their use is always special, but descriptions of this meal are bewilderingly varied. Even today, when Christians are more conscious of their common faith than they have been for centuries, differences in eucharistic faith and practice continue to divide them. In this study, the authors combine a history of this Christian meal and an analysis of the present situation to illuminate proposals for a way forward. They insist that Christians must understand each others' views in the light of the Bible's teaching before all who break the one bread can really share it as one body.